THE GRAYWOLF ANN

MULTI-CULTURAL LITERACY

1988

THE GRAYWOLF ANNUAL FIVE: MULTI-CULTURAL LITERACY

Edited by Rick Simonson
& Scott Walker

GRAYWOLF PRESS: SAINT PAUL

Publication of this volume is made possible in part by grants from the National Endowment for the Arts, the Minnesota State Arts Board, and very generous contributions from corporations, foundations, and individuals. Graywolf Press is a member organization of United Arts, Saint Paul.

Cover: "Cowhead Discovers Human Beings" is a quilt by Amy Cordova.
The design is based on the journals of Cabeza de Vaca,
Adventures in the Unknown Interior of America.
(Photo by Robert Brace)

ISBN 1-55597-114-8
ISSN 0743-7471

Set in Baskerville

Published by GRAYWOLF PRESS
Post Office Box 75006, Saint Paul, Minnesota 55175.

ACKNOWLEDGMENTS

The essays collected in this Graywolf Annual have appeared previously in publications, as noted below. We gratefully acknowledge the cooperation of editors, agents, and the authors for their permission to reprint the essays here.

Paula Gunn Allen's "Who Is Your Mother? Red Roots of Feminism" is from *The Sacred Hoop: Recovering the Feminine in American Indian Traditions* (Beacon Press, 1986). Copyright © 1986 by Paula Gunn Allen.

Gloria Anzaldúa's *"Tlilli, Tlapalli:* The Path of the Red and Black Ink" is from *Borderlands/La Frontera: The New Mestiza* (Spinsters/Aunt Lute, 1987). Copyright © 1987 by Gloria Anzaldúa.

James Baldwin's "A Talk to Teachers" was originally delivered on October 16, 1963, as "The Negro Child – His Self-Image" and originally published in *The Saturday Review,* December 21, 1963, then published in a collection of essays, *The Price of the Ticket* (St. Martin's Press, 1985). Copyright © 1985 by James Baldwin.

Wendell Berry's "People, Land, and Community" is from *Standing by Words: Essays* (North Point Press, 1983). Copyright © 1983 by Wendell Berry.

Michelle Cliff's "A Journey into Speech" and "If I Could Write This in Fire, I Would Write This in Fire" is from *The Land of Look Behind* (Firebrand Books, 1985). Copyright © 1985 by Michelle Cliff.

Carlos Fuentes's "The Discovery of Mexico" was originally published in *Granta,* then was included in *Myself with Others* and entitled "How I Started to Write" (Farrar, Straus and Giroux, Inc., 1988). Copyright © 1981, 1983, 1986, 1988 by Carlos Fuentes.

Eduardo Galeano's "In Defense of the Word" is from *Days and Nights of Love and War,* translated by Bobbye S. Ortiz (Monthly Review Press, 1983). Copyright © 1983 by Monthly Review Press.

Guillermo Gómez-Peña's "Documented/Undocumented" is from the *L.A. Weekly,* translated by Ruben Martinez. Copyright © 1988 by Guillermo Gómez-Peña.

David Mura's "Strangers in the Village" is published here for the first time. Copyright © 1988 by David Mura.

Ishmael Reed's "America: The Multinational Society" was originally published in *San Francisco Focus* and then was published in *Writin' Is Fightin'* (Atheneum Publishers, an imprint of Macmillan Publishing Co., 1988). Copyright © 1988 by Ishmael Reed.

Michael Ventura's "Report from El Dorado" is from *Shadow Dancing in the U.S.A.* (Jeremy Tarcher, 1985). Copyright © 1985 by Michael Ventura.

Michele Wallace's "Invisibility Blues" was first published in *Zeta* magazine (Institute for Social & Cultural Communications, 1987). Copyright © 1987 Michele Wallace.

CONTENTS

The Graywolf Annual 5
is dedicated to

JAMES BALDWIN
&
JOSEPH CAMPBELL.

The editors are grateful to many people
for their help in compiling this anthology.
Among those whose aid and encouragement
have been invaluable are:

Toni Cade Bambara
Page Cowles
Tim Fisher
Rebecca Mark
David Mura
Barbara Thomas
&
the staff at Elliott Bay Books

INTRODUCTION

In 1987, two serious books about American education became surprise best-sellers and the focal points of a renewed
national debate about values and education. To date, the two
books have sold nearly two million copies. The books are,
simultaneously, impassioned pleas for making education a
higher priority and blueprints for the revival of a conservative system of education utterly out of date with contemporary cultural and political realities.

Allan Bloom's *The Closing of the American Mind* is a "lack of"
book, a book that complains of contemporary America's lack
of values, our educational system's lack of purpose, and the
average American's lack of vision, lack of understanding, and
lack of knowledge. Bloom seems to long for a Reaganesque
return to simpler times, when men were men, when we all –
meaning white folk more than colored, meaning more men
than women – learned the 3-R's by way of the certain classic
texts, in our little schoolhouses on the prairies.

E. D. Hirsch, Jr.'s *Cultural Literacy* gives alarming examples
of high school and college graduates' ignorance of what Hirsch
perceives to be the "basic" terms, facts, and concepts of our
culture. He argues for a "return" to a system of education
that teaches all citizens an established vocabulary of culture,
so that we can talk together using the same system of cultural
referents.

Hirsch's examples – the high school boy who, when asked
to name an epic poem by Homer, answered, "The Alamo!";
the college junior who thought Toronto was a city in Italy; the
alarming decline in college entrance examination scores –
provided thundering first paragraphs to editorial writers
across the U.S. Hirsch, Joseph Katt, and James Trefil compiled a list of 5,000 things, names, proverbs, quotes, and
concepts that "literate Americans know."

The renewed national debate about education and values has become something of a fad, which started in 1986 on publication of Jonathan Kozol's *Illiterate America,* a book that delivered the disturbing news that one in six of us can't read the Surgeon General's warnings or know what we're going to eat for dinner before opening the can. The books by Hirsch and Bloom settled onto bestseller lists in hardcover and paperback. William Bennett, President Reagan's former Secretary of Education, has for years stumped cross-country advocating "back-to-basics" education. Duke University's and Stanford University's amendments to their core reading lists became a national controversy. Stanford's previous "Western Culture Program," with its Eurocentric, exclusively male list of authors, will in the future give way to a "Cultures, Values, and Ideas Program" which broadens in gender and national origin the list of great books read as part of a student's fundamental education.

The editors of this *Graywolf Annual* agree with Hirsch, Bloom, and the editorial writers of America that education should be among the highest of national priorities, and that our current educational system is desperately wanting of both vision and financing. The need for change is urgent.

We do take issue with Hirsch's and Bloom's definitions of what (or whose) culture should be taught. We are alarmed by the number of people who are so enthusiastically in agreement with the Hirsch/Bloom argument for educational reform that they fail to discern its overridingly static, and so shallow, definition of culture. Both writers seem to think that most of what constitutes contemporary American and world culture was immaculately conceived by a few men in Greece, around 900 B.C., came to its full expression in Europe a few centuries later, and began to decline around the middle of the nineteenth century.

Much of the Hirsch/Bloom world view is outdated. Most Americans are now aware of the contributions of repressed cultures, more alert to how history has been rewritten and molded to the vision of the majority population, and accustomed to the notion that culture, like language, changes, and that we ought to be sensitive to those changes. Though Hirsch is right, as far as he goes, in his list of 5,000 things that savvy folk ought to know, he doesn't go far or deep enough. We need to know much more.

America's historians have enjoyed thinking of the country as a melting pot into which all ethnic populations thoroughly mixed. This may have been a faulty notion in the first place, and it is certainly no longer true. Here, as elsewhere in the world, ethnic, minority populations (usually defined as "people of color"; and in many places actually the majority population) find ways to succeed within the mainstream culture while at the same time proudly preserving their own languages and cultures. Exemplifying this trend are the growing Latino population in the United States, particularly in New York and the Southwest; the more recently arrived Southeast Asian population; the identity-seeking revival of Germanic and Nordic traditions among people long since considered fully "melted" Americans; and the admirable re-culturing of the American Indians. At a time when one in four Americans are people of color, none of us can afford to remain ignorant of the heritage and culture of any part of our population. Watching Jesse Jackson's political campaigns, as the Rainbow Coalition's broad appeal finds common ground, we have witnessed the development of a new definition of what comprises "mainstream" culture.

The twentieth century revolution in communications, the rise and pervasiveness of mass media, and dramatic changes in the world economy have led to a softening of political and cultural boundaries. As the world is "made smaller" and cultures become more uniform (imperialism taking on cultural as well as political forms), we are simultaneously brought closer together and suffer the destruction of individual languages, imagination, and cultural meaning. As we learn more about ecology and of ways to preserve nature, we should also learn the great value of diversity and seek to preserve a diverse cultural heritage. Economic development has historically led

the way to cultural expansion. As the world becomes more of
a single economic entity, there is a corresponding need for all
citizens to have not only a fundamental understanding of
their own culture (in part to conserve it), but also a knowledge
of the cultures of the rest of the world. However, the citizens
of the United States are profoundly ignorant of world litera-
tures, histories, mythologies, and politics. For the United
States to continue to have cultural and economic relevance,
this inadequacy must be addressed.

2

Hirsch, Katt, and Trefil admit to knowing they were asking
for trouble by compiling their list, "What Literate Americans
Know." The list (which in its revised paperback edition is still
called "preliminary") is peculiarly and appropriately wide-
ranging. It includes *the Beatles, weather map, realpolitik, A rolling
stone gathers no moss, Verdi, Bronze Age, tectonic plates,* and *Ty
Cobb.* But Hirsch is disturbingly ignorant of some very common aspects of culture.

Women, for example. Though Hirsch's list does include
penis envy, macho, and *vasectomy,* he fails to find significant
mastectomy, gynecology, or *Georgia O'Keeffe.* Nor does he deem it
important for culturally literate Americans to know about
*alcoholism, internment camps, Bhagavad Gita, Pele, rhythm and
blues, computer crash, El Salvador,* or *One Hundred Years of Solitude.* Hirsch doesn't seem to consider it of value for Americans to know about food and agriculture, the environment,
world geography, non-European history, or the plants and
animals with whom we share the planet. Some of these omis-
sions are the result of oversight. Many result from a particular white, male, academic, eastern U.S., Eurocentric bias that
severely limits Hirsch's and Bloom's and Reagan's and Bennett's concept of American culture.

Despite our own best judgment, the editors of this anthology have compiled the beginnings of a list of words, concepts,
names, and titles that were omitted by Hirsch and Co. Our

list, presented as an appendix to this volume, is offered simply to show some aspects of our culture that are not deemed significant by our more conservative educators and policy makers. These educators and politicians form U.S. educational policy, and therefore our future, and they too often ignore the part that women and/or people of color play in making this culture and country what it is.

3

In researching material for this anthology, the editors spoke to many people who for years have thought and written about issues of multi-culturalism, the history of civilizations, feminist literature and culture, ethnicity, and the literature and histories of many non-White and non-European cultures. It was surprising to find how few of these people knew about either the Bloom or the Hirsch books. When informed of the books, most dismissed them as hapless throwbacks to a more conservative time. The issues of the contributions to our culture made by women and people of color, and of the importance of developing a worldwide view of culture, had, to these people, been settled years ago.

Clearly, though, the issues of what our culture is and how it can be taught have not been settled. They have not been settled in the academic world nor in the everyday world in which we all live and work. Americans need to have a better grasp of the European heritage and a clearer understanding of American history and culture, to know its depths and soul. Americans need to broaden their awareness and understanding of the cultures of the rest of the world. Other histories and cultures reveal ancestry and knowledge that has bearing on who we are and where we are going. By understanding more about our immediate locale, the native soil we stand on and the other living things that share our world, we expand our imaginations and expand our culture. The language of the academic world, of government, of business, of mass media so easily becomes abstract, distancing, manipulative.

Such language cannot, with its nervous speed, its strip-mind, appropriating qualities, touch the deep, turned-over ground of our culture. Such language can, and often does, seek to bury it.

4

Most of the essays presented in this *Graywolf Annual* were written before the appearance of either *Cultural Literacy* or *The Closing of the American Mind.* Chronologically, they range as far back as James Baldwin's talk to a group of teachers twenty-five years ago. Though we are putting them in a new context by assembling them here, all of these writers are accustomed to looking at this culture from both particular and broader viewpoints. We encourage those who like what they find here to read further. Several of the essays come from books these writers have published which tackle questions of self, society, art, community, and culture.

For ourselves, the desire to compile this anthology comes from an engaged, everyday view of this society. Both of the editors of this anthology work in the world of books, as a bookseller and as a publisher. We know that culture is largely contained and carried in the word, and also that it has to swim in perilous seas, against a tide of many false-cultured words and images. One has responsibilities. Getting good writing into the hands of readers is a fundamental one. We are pleased to do that with the essays included here.

Still more to the heart of why the editors began to assemble this particular *Graywolf Annual* was a reading of James Baldwin's *The Price of the Ticket,* undertaken this past winter. James Baldwin – like Joseph Campbell, another whose writing moved deeply beyond all sorts of artificially made barriers – died in the fall of 1987. In tribute, there were loving reminiscences, stories, and testaments by writers such as Toni Morrison, Amiri Baraka, Maya Angelou, William Styron, Chinua Achebe, Sonia Sanchez, and John Edgar Wideman, among others. Baldwin's great *The Price of the Ticket,* which collects his nonfiction writing from 1948–1985, was read against the backdrop of the brouhaha caused by the publication of the Hirsch and Bloom books, the hubbub over the change in Stanford's core curriculum, and National Endowment for the Humanities Chair Lynne Cheney's pronouncements about how the government was doing too much for women and minorities. The national media, in an election year, again and again brought up the question of what Jesse Jackson and his followers really "want." James Baldwin wrote powerfully of this country's identity and soul, and the love, fear, anger, dreams, and pain carried therein. James Baldwin fixed the responsibility for how we live with each of us. It is to his memory and work – and that of Joseph Campbell – that we dedicate this collection.

Rick Simonson and Scott Walker
Seattle and Saint Paul
July 1988

THE GRAYWOLF ANNUAL FIVE:

MULTI-CULTURAL LITERACY

1988

JAMES BALDWIN

A Talk to Teachers

Let's begin by saying that we are living through a very dangerous time. Everyone in this room is in one way or another aware of that. We are in a revolutionary situation, no matter how unpopular that word has become in this country. The society in which we live is desperately menaced, not by Khrushchev, but from within. So any citizen of this country who figures himself as responsible – and particularly those of you who deal with the minds and hearts of young people – must be prepared to "go for broke." Or to put it another way, you must understand that in the attempt to correct so many generations of bad faith and cruelty, when it is operating not only in the classroom but in society, you will meet the most fantastic, the most brutal, and the most determined resistance. There is no point in pretending that this won't happen.

Since I am talking to schoolteachers and I am not a teacher myself, and in some ways am fairly easily intimidated, I beg you to let me leave that and go back to what I think to be the entire purpose of education in the first place. It would seem to me that when a child is born, if I'm the child's parent, it is my obligation and my high duty to civilize that child. Man is a social animal. He cannot exist without a society. A society, in turn, depends on certain things which everyone within that society takes for granted. Now, the crucial paradox which

confronts us here is that the whole process of education occurs within a social framework and is designed to perpetuate
the aims of society. Thus, for example, the boys and girls who
were born during the era of the Third Reich, when educated
to the purposes of the Third Reich, became barbarians. The
paradox of education is precisely this – that as one begins to
become conscious one begins to examine the society in which
he is being educated. The purpose of education, finally, is to
create in a person the ability to look at the world for himself,
to make his own decisions, to say to himself this is black or this
is white, to decide for himself whether there is a God in
heaven or not. To ask questions of the universe, and then
learn to live with those questions, is the way he achieves his
own identity. But no society is really anxious to have that kind
of person around. What societies really, ideally, want is a citi-
zenry which will simply obey the rules of society. If a society
succeeds in this, that society is about to perish. The obligation
of anyone who thinks of himself as responsible is to examine
society and try to change it and to fight it – at no matter what
risk. This is the only hope society has. This is the only way
societies change.

Now, if what I have tried to sketch has any validity, it becomes thoroughly clear, at least to me, that any Negro who is
born in this country and undergoes the American educational
system runs the risk of becoming schizophrenic. On the one
hand he is born in the shadow of the stars and stripes and he
is assured it represents a nation which has never lost a war.
He pledges allegiance to that flag which guarantees "liberty
and justice for all." He is part of a country in which anyone
can become president, and so forth. But on the other hand he
is also assured by his country and his countrymen that he has
never contributed anything to civilization – that his past is
nothing more than a record of humiliations gladly endured.
He is assumed by the republic that he, his father, his mother,
and his ancestors were happy, shiftless, watermelon-eating
darkies who loved Mr. Charlie and Miss Ann, that the value

he has as a black man is proven by one thing only – his devotion to white people. If you think I am exaggerating, examine the myths which proliferate in this country about Negroes.

All this enters the child's consciousness much sooner than we as adults would like to think it does. As adults, we are easily fooled because we are so anxious to be fooled. But children are very different. Children, not yet aware that it is dangerous to look too deeply at anything, look at everything, look at each other, and draw their own conclusions. They don't have the vocabulary to express what they see, and we, their elders, know how to intimidate them very easily and very soon. But a black child, looking at the world around him, though he cannot know quite what to make of it, is aware that there is a reason why his mother works so hard, why his father is always on edge. He is aware that there is some reason why, if he sits down in the front of the bus, his father or mother slaps him and drags him to the back of the bus. He is aware that there is some terrible weight on his parents' shoulders which menaces him. And it isn't long – in fact it begins when he is in school – before he discovers the shape of his oppression.

Let us say that the child is seven years old and I am his father, and I decide to take him to the zoo, or to Madison Square Garden, or to the U.N. Building, or to any of the tremendous monuments we find all over New York. We get into a bus and we go from where I live on 131st Street and Seventh Avenue downtown through the park and we get into New York City, which is not Harlem. Now, where the boy lives – even if it is a housing project – is in an undesirable neighborhood. If he lives in one of those housing projects of which everyone in New York is so proud, he has at the front door, if not closer, the pimps, the whores, the junkies – in a word, the danger of life in the ghetto. And the child knows this, though he doesn't know why.

I still remember my first sight of New York. It was really another city when I was born – where I was born. We looked down over the Park Avenue streetcar tracks. It was Park Avenue, but I didn't know what Park Avenue meant *downtown*. The Park Avenue I grew up on, which is still standing, is dark and dirty. No one would dream of opening a Tiffany's on that Park Avenue, and when you go downtown you discover that you are literally in the white world. It is rich – or at least it looks rich. It is clean – because they collect garbage downtown. There are doormen. People walk about as though they owned where they are – and indeed they do. And it's a great shock. It's very hard to relate yourself to this. You don't know what it means. You know – you know instinctively – that none of this is for you. You know this before you are told. And who is it for and who is paying for it? And why isn't it for you?

Later on when you become a grocery boy or messenger and you try to enter one of those buildings a man says, "Go to the back door." Still later, if you happen by some odd chance to have a friend in one of those buildings, the man says, "Where's your package?" Now this by no means is the core of the matter. What I'm trying to get at is that by this time the Negro child has had, effectively, almost all the doors of opportunity slammed in his face, and there are very few things he can do about it. He can more or less accept it with an absolutely inarticulate and dangerous rage inside – all the more dangerous because it is never expressed. It is precisely those silent people whom white people see every day of their lives – I mean your porter and your maid, who never say anything more than "Yes, Sir" and "No, Ma'am." They will tell you it's raining if that is what you want to hear, and they will tell you the sun is shining if *that* is what you want to hear. They really hate you – really hate you because in their eyes (and they're right) you stand between them and life. I want to come back to that in a moment. It is the most sinister of the facts, I think, which we now face.

There is something else the Negro child can do, too. Every street boy – and I was a street boy, so I know – looking at the society which has produced him, looking at the standards of that society which are not honored by anybody, looking at your churches and the government and the politicians, understands that this structure is operated for someone else's benefit – not for his. And there's no reason in it for him. If he is really cunning, really ruthless, really strong – and many of us are – he becomes a kind of criminal. He becomes a kind of criminal because that's the only way he can live. Harlem and every ghetto in this city – every ghetto in this country – is full of people who live outside the law. They wouldn't dream of calling a policeman. They wouldn't, for a moment, listen to any of those professions of which we are so proud on the Fourth of July. They have turned away from this country forever and totally. They live by their wits and really long to see the day when the entire structure comes down.

The point of all this is that black men were brought here as a source of cheap labor. They were indispensable to the economy. In order to justify the fact that men were treated as though they were animals, the white republic had to brainwash itself into believing that they were, indeed, animals and *deserved* to be treated like animals. Therefore it is almost impossible for any Negro child to discover anything about his actual history. The reason is that this "animal," once he suspects his own worth, once he starts believing that he is a man, has begun to attack the entire power structure. This is why America has spent such a long time keeping the Negro in his place. What I am trying to suggest to you is that it was not an accident, it was not an act of God, it was not done by well-meaning people muddling into something which they didn't understand. It was a deliberate policy hammered into place in order to make money from black flesh. And now, in 1963, because we have never faced this fact, we are in intolerable trouble.

The Reconstruction, as I read the evidence, was a bargain between the North and South to this effect: "We've liberated them from the land – and delivered them to the bosses." When we left Mississippi to come North we did not come to freedom. We came to the bottom of the labor market, and we are still there. Even the Depression of the 1930s failed to make a dent in Negroes' relationship to white workers in the labor unions. Even today, so brainwashed is this republic that people seriously ask in what they suppose to be good faith, "What does the Negro want?" I've heard a great many asinine questions in my life, but that is perhaps the most asinine and perhaps the most insulting. But the point here is that people who ask that question, thinking that they ask it in good faith, are really the victims of this conspiracy to make Negroes believe they are less than human.

In order for me to live, I decided very early that some mistake had been made somewhere. I was not a "nigger" even though you called me one. But if I was a "nigger" in your eyes, there was something about *you* – there was something *you* needed. I had to realize when I was very young that I was none of those things I was told I was. I was not, for example, happy. I never touched a watermelon for all kinds of reasons that had been invented by white people, and I knew enough about life by this time to understand that whatever you invent, whatever you project, is you! So where we are now is that a whole country of people believe I'm a "nigger," and I *don't*, and the battle's on! Because if I am not what I've been told I am, then it means that *you're* not what you thought *you* were *either*! And that is the crisis.

It is not really a "Negro revolution" that is upsetting the country. What is upsetting the country is a sense of its own identity. If, for example, one managed to change the curriculum in all the schools so that Negroes learned more about themselves and their real contributions to this culture, you would be liberating not only Negroes, you'd be liberating white people who know nothing about their own history. And the reason is that if you are compelled to lie about one aspect of anybody's history, you must lie about it all. If you have to lie about my real role here, if you have to pretend that I hoed all that cotton just because I loved you, then you have done something to yourself. You are mad.

Now let's go back a minute. I talked earlier about those

silent people – the porter and the maid – who, as I said, don't look up at the sky if you ask them if it is raining, but look into your face. My ancestors and I were very well trained. We understood very early that this was not a Christian nation. It didn't matter what you said or how often you went to church. My father and my mother and my grandfather and my grandmother knew that Christians didn't act this way. It was as simple as that. And if that was so there was no point in dealing with white people in terms of their own moral professions, for they were not going to honor them. What one did was to turn away, smiling all the time, and tell white people what they wanted to hear. But people always accuse you of reckless talk when you say this.

All this means that there are in this country tremendous reservoirs of bitterness which have never been able to find an outlet, but may find an outlet soon. It means that well-meaning white liberals place themselves in great danger when they try to deal with Negroes as though they were missionaries. It means, in brief, that a great price is demanded to liberate all those silent people so that they can breathe for the first time and *tell* you what they think of you. And a price is demanded to liberate all those white children – some of them near forty – who have never grown up, and who never will grow up, because they have no sense of their identity.

What passes for identity in America is a series of myths about one's heroic ancestors. It's astounding to me, for example, that so many people really appear to believe that the country was founded by a band of heroes who wanted to be free. That happens not to be true. What happened was that some people left Europe because they couldn't stay there any longer and had to go someplace else to make it. That's all. They were hungry, they were poor, they were convicts. Those who were making it in England, for example, did not get on the *Mayflower*. That's how the country was settled. Not by Gary Cooper. Yet we have a whole race of people, a whole republic, who believe the myths to the point where even today they select political representatives, as far as I can tell, by how closely they resemble Gary Cooper. Now this is dangerously infantile, and it shows in every level of national life. When I was living in Europe, for example, one of the worst revelations to me was the way Americans walked around Europe buying this and buying that and insulting everybody – not even out of malice, just because they didn't know any better. Well, that is the way they have always treated me. They weren't cruel, they just didn't know you were alive. They didn't know you had any feelings.

What I am trying to suggest here is that in the doing of all this for 100 years or more, it is the American white man who has long since lost his grip on reality. In some peculiar way, having created this myth about Negroes, and the myth about his own history, he created myths about the world so that, for example, he was astounded that some people could prefer Castro, astounded that there are people in the world who don't go into hiding when they hear the word "Communism," astounded that Communism is one of the realities of the twentieth century which we will not overcome by pretending that it does not exist. The political level in this country now, on the part of people who should know better, is abysmal.

The Bible says somewhere that where there is no vision the people perish. I don't think anyone can doubt that in this country today we are menaced – intolerably menaced – by a lack of vision.

It is inconceivable that a sovereign people should continue, as we do so abjectly, to say, "I can't do anything about it. It's the government." The government is the creation of the people. It is responsible to the people. And the people are responsible for it. No American has the right to allow the present government to say, when Negro children are being bombed and hosed and shot and beaten all over the Deep South, that there is nothing we can do about it. There must have been a day in this country's life when the bombing of the children in Sunday School would have created a public uproar and endangered the life of a Governor Wallace. It happened here and there was no public uproar.

I began by saying that one of the paradoxes of education was that precisely at the point when you begin to develop a conscience, you must find yourself at war with your society. It is your responsibility to change society if you think of yourself as an educated person. And on the basis of the evidence – the moral and political evidence – one is compelled to say that this is a backward society. Now if I were a teacher in this school, or any Negro school, and I was dealing with Negro children, who were in my care only a few hours of every day and would then return to their homes and to the streets, children who have an apprehension of their future which with every hour grows grimmer and darker, I would try to teach them – I would try to make them know – that those streets, those houses, those dangers, those agonies by which they are surrounded, are criminal. I would try to make each child know that these things are the result of a criminal conspiracy to destroy him. I would teach him that if he intends to get to be a man, he must at once decide that he is stronger than this conspiracy and that he must never make his peace with it. And that one of his weapons for refusing to make his peace with it and for destroying it depends on what he decides he is worth. I would teach him that there are currently very few standards in this country which are worth a man's respect. That it is up to him to begin to change these standards for the sake of the life and the health of the country. I would suggest to him that the popular culture – as represented, for example, on television and in comic books and in movies – is based on fantasies created by very ill people, and he must be aware that these are fantasies that have nothing to do with reality. I would teach him that the press he reads is not as free as it says it is – and that he can do something about that, too. I would try to make him know that just as American history is longer, larger, more various, more beautiful, and more terrible than anything anyone has ever said about it, so is the world larger,

more daring, more beautiful and more terrible, but princi-
pally larger – and that it belongs to him. I would teach him
that he doesn't have to be bound by the expediencies of any
given administration, any given policy, any given morality;
that he has the right and the necessity to examine everything.
I would try to show him that one has not learned anything
about Castro when one says, "He is a Communist." This is a
way of his learning something about Castro, something about
Cuba, something, in time, about the world. I would suggest to
him that he is living, at the moment, in an enormous province. America is not the world and if America is going to
become a nation, she must find a way – and this child must
help her to find a way to use the tremendous potential and
tremendous energy which this child represents. If this country does not find a way to use that energy, it will be destroyed
by that energy.

PAULA GUNN ALLEN

Who Is Your Mother?
Red Roots of White Feminism

At Laguna Pueblo in New Mexico, "Who is your mother?" is an important question. At Laguna, one of several of the ancient Keres gynocratic societies of the region, your mother's identity is the key to your own identity. Among the Keres, every individual has a place within the universe – human and nonhuman – and that place is defined by clan membership. In turn, clan membership is dependent on matrilineal descent. Of course, your mother is not only that woman whose womb formed and released you – the term refers in every individual case to an entire generation of women whose psychic, and consequently physical, "shape" made the psychic existence of the following generation possible. But naming your own mother (or her equivalent) enables people to place you precisely within the universal web of your life, in each of its dimensions: cultural, spiritual, personal, and historical.

Among the Keres, "context" and "matrix" are equivalent terms, and both refer to approximately the same thing as knowing your derivation and place. Failure to know your mother, that is, your position and its attendant traditions, history, and place in the scheme of things, is failure to remember your significance, your reality, your right relationship to earth and society. It is the same thing as being lost – isolated, abandoned, self-estranged, and alienated from your own life. This importance of tradition in the life of every member of the community is not confined to Keres Indians; all American Indian Nations place great value on traditionalism.

The Native American sense of the importance of continuity with one's cultural origins runs counter to contemporary American ideas: in many instances, the immigrants to America have been eager to cast off cultural ties, often seeing their antecedents as backward, restrictive, even shameful. Rejection of tradition constitutes one of the major features of American life, an attitude that reaches far back into American colonial history and that now is validated by virtually every cultural institution in the country. Feminist practice, at least in the cultural artifacts the community values most, follows this cultural trend as well.

The American idea that the best and the brightest should willingly reject and repudiate their origins leads to an allied idea – that history, like everything in the past, is of little value and should be forgotten as quickly as possible. This all too often causes us to reinvent the wheel continually. We find ourselves discovering our collective pasts over and over, having to retake ground already covered by women in the preceding decades and centuries. The Native American view, which highly values maintenance of traditional customs, values, and perspectives, might result in slower societal change and in quite a bit less social upheaval, but it has the advantage of providing a solid sense of identity and lowered levels of psychological and interpersonal conflict.

Contemporary Indian communities value individual members who are deeply connected to the traditional ways of their people, even after centuries of concerted and brutal effort on the part of the American government, the churches, and the corporate system to break the connections between individuals and their tribal world. In fact, in the view of the traditionals, rejection of one's culture – one's traditions, language, people – is the result of colonial oppression and is hardly to be applauded. They believe that the roots of oppression are to be found in the loss of tradition and memory because that loss is always accompanied by a loss of a positive sense of self. In short, Indians think it is important to remember, while Americans believe it is important to forget.

The traditional Indians' view can have a significant impact if it is expanded to mean that the sources of social, political, and philosophical thought in the Americas not only should be recognized and honored by Native Americans but should be embraced by American society. If American society judiciously modeled the traditions of the various Native Nations, the place of women in society would become central, the distribution of goods and power would be egalitarian, the elderly would be respected, honored, and protected as a primary social and cultural resource, the ideals of physical beauty would be considerably enlarged (to include "fat," strong-featured women, gray-haired, and wrinkled individuals, and others who in contemporary American culture are viewed as "ugly"). Additionally, the destruction of the biota, the life sphere, and the natural resources of the planet would be curtailed, and the spiritual nature of human and nonhuman life would become a primary organizing principle of human society. And if the traditional tribal systems that are emulated included pacifist ones, war would cease to be a major method of human problem solving.

Re-membering Connections and Histories

The belief that rejection of tradition and of history is a useful reponse to life is reflected in America's amazing loss of memory concerning its origins in the matrix and context of Native America. America does not seem to remember that it derived its wealth, its values, its food, much of its medicine, and a large part of its "dream" from Native America. It is ignorant of the genesis of its culture in this Native American land, and that ignorance helps to perpetuate the long-standing European and Middle Eastern monotheistic, hierarchical, patriarchal cultures' oppression of women, gays, and lesbians, people of color, working class, unemployed people, and the elderly. Hardly anyone in America speculates that the constitutional system of government might be as much a product of American Indian ideas and practices as of colonial American and Anglo-European revolutionary fervor.

Even though Indians are officially and informally ignored as intellectual movers and shapers in the United States, Britain, and Europe, they are peoples with ancient tenure on this soil. During the ages when tribal societies existed in the Americas largely untouched by patriarchal oppression, they developed elaborate systems of thought that included science, philosophy, and government based on a belief in the central importance of female energies, autonomy of individuals, co-operation, human dignity, human freedom, and egalitarian distribution of status, goods, and services. Respect for others, reverence for life, and, as a by-product, pacifism as a way of life; importance of kinship ties in the customary ordering of social interaction; a sense of the sacredness and mystery of existence; balance and harmony in relationships both sacred and secular were all features of life among the tribal confederacies and nations. And in those that lived by the largest number of these principles, gynarchy was the norm rather than the exception. Those systems are as yet unmatched in any contemporary industrial, agrarian, or postindustrial society on earth.

There are many female gods recognized and honored by the tribes and Nations. Femaleness was highly valued, both respected and feared, and all social institutions reflected this attitude. Even modern sayings, such as the Cheyenne statement that a people is not conquered until the hearts of the women are on the ground, express the Indians' understanding that without the power of woman the people will not live, but with it, they will endure and prosper.

Indians did not confine this belief in the central importance of female energy to matters of worship. Among many of the tribes (perhaps as many as 70 percent of them in North America alone), this belief was reflected in all of their social institutions. The Iroquois Constitution or White Roots of Peace, also called the Great Law of the Iroquois, codified the Matrons' decision-making and economic power:

> The lineal descent of the people of the Five Fires [the Iroquois Nations] shall run in the female line. Women shall be considered the progenitors of the Nation. They shall own the land and the soil. Men and women shall follow the status of their mothers. (Article 44)
>
> The women heirs of the chieftainship titles of the League shall be called Oiner or Otinner [Noble] for all time to come. (Article 45)
>
> If a disobedient chief persists in his disobedience after three warnings [by his female relatives, by his male relatives, and by one of his fellow council members, in that order], the matter shall go to the council of War Chiefs. The Chiefs shall then take away the title of the erring chief *by order of the women in whom the title is vested.* When the chief is deposed, the women shall notify the chiefs of the League ... and the chiefs of the League shall sanction the act. The women will then select another of their sons as a candidate and the chiefs shall elect him. (Article 19) (Emphasis mine) [1]

The Matrons held so much policy-making power traditionally that once, when their position was threatened they demanded its return, and consequently the power of women was fundamental in shaping the Iroquois Confederation sometime in the sixteenth or early seventeenth century. It was women

> who fought what may have been the first successful feminist rebellion in the New World. The year was 1600, or thereabouts, when these tribal feminists decided that they had had enough of unregulated warfare by their men. Lysistratas among the Indian women proclaimed a boycott on lovemaking and childbearing. Until the men conceded to them the power to decide upon war and peace, there would be no more warriors. Since the men believed that the women alone knew the secret of childbirth, the rebellion was instantly successful.

In the Constitution of Deganawidah the founder of the Iroquois Confederation of Nations had said: "He caused the body of our mother, the woman, to be of great worth and honor. He purposed that she shall be endowed and entrusted with the birth and upbringing of men, and that she shall have the care of all that is planted by which life is sustained and supported and the power to breathe is fortified: *and moreover that the warriors shall be her assistants.*"

The footnote of history was curiously supplied when Susan B. Anthony began her "Votes for Women" movement two and a half centuries later. Unknowingly the feminists chose to hold their founding convention of latter-day suffragettes in the town of Seneca [Falls], New York. The site was just a stone's throw from the old council house where the Iroquois women had plotted their feminist rebellion. (Emphasis mine)[2]

Beliefs, attitudes, and laws such as these became part of the vision of American feminists and of other human liberation movements around the world. Yet feminists too often believe that no one has ever experienced the kind of society that empowered women and made that empowerment the basis of its rules of civilization. The price the feminist community must pay because it is not aware of the recent presence of gynarchical societies on this continent is unnecessary confusion, division, and much lost time.

The Root of Oppression Is Loss of Memory

An odd thing occurs in the minds of Americans when Indian civilization is mentioned: little or nothing. As I write this, I am aware of how far removed my version of the roots of American feminism must seem to those steeped in either mainstream or radical versions of feminism's history. I am keenly aware of the lack of image Americans have about our continent's recent past. I am intensely conscious of popular notions of Indian women as beasts of burden, squaws, traitors, or, at best, vanished denizens of a long-lost wilderness. How odd, then, must my contention seem that the gynocratic tribes of the American continent provided the basis for all the dreams of liberation that characterize the modern world.

We as feminists must be aware of our history on this continent. We need to recognize that the same forces that devastated the gynarchies of Britain and the Continent also devastated the ancient African civilizations, and we must know that those same materialistic, antispiritual forces are presently engaged in wiping out the same gynarchical values, along with the peoples who adhere to them, in Latin America. I am convinced that those wars were and continue to be about the imposition of patriarchal civilization over the holistic, pacifist, and spirit-based gynarchies they supplant. To that end the wars of imperial conquest have not been solely or even mostly waged over the land and its resources, but they have been fought within the bodies, minds, and hearts of the people of the earth for dominion over them. I think this is the reason traditionals say we must remember our origins, our cultures, our histories, our mothers and grandmothers, for without that memory, which implies continuance rather than nostalgia, we are doomed to engulfment by a paradigm that is fundamentally inimical to the vitality, autonomy, and self-empowerment essential for satisfying, high-quality life.

The vision that impels feminists to action was the vision of the Grandmothers' society, the society that was captured in the words of the sixteenth-century explorer Peter Martyr nearly five hundred years ago. It is the same vision repeated over and over by radical thinkers of Europe and America, from François Villon to John Locke, from William Shakespeare to Thomas Jefferson, from Karl Marx to Friedrich Engels, from Benito Juarez to Martin Luther King, from Elizabeth Cady Stanton to Judy Grahn, from Harriet Tubman to Audre Lorde, from Emma Goldman to Bella Abzug, from Malinalli to Cherrie Moraga, and from Iyatiku to me. That vision as Martyr told it is of a country where there are "no soldiers, no gendarmes or police, no nobles, kings, regents, prefects, or judges, no prisons, no lawsuits ... All are equal and free," or so Friedrich Engels recounts Martyr's words.[3]

Columbus wrote:

> Nor have I been able to learn whether they [the inhabitants
> of the islands he visited on his first journey to the New World]
> held personal property, for it seemed to me that whatever one
> had, they all took shares of . . . They are so ingenuous and free
> with all they have, that no one would believe it who has not seen
> it; of anything that they possess, if it be asked of them, they
> never say no; on the contrary, they invite you to share it and
> show as much love as if their hearts went with it.[4]

At least that's how the Native Caribbean people acted when
the whites first came among them; American Indians are the
despair of social workers, bosses, and missionaries even now
because of their deeply ingrained tendency to spend all they
have, mostly on others. In any case, as the historian William
Brandon notes,

> the Indian *seemed* free, to European eyes, gloriously free, to the
> European soul shaped by centuries of toil and tyranny, and this
> impression operated profoundly on the process of history and
> the development of America. Something in the peculiar char-
> acter of the Indian world gave an impression of classlessness,
> of propertylessness, and that in turn led to an impression, as
> H. H. Bancroft put it, of "humanity unrestrained . . . in the
> exercise of liberty absolute."[5]

A Feminist Heroine

Early in the women's suffrage movement, Eva Emery Dye, an
Oregon suffragette, went looking for a heroine to embody
her vision of feminism. She wanted a historical figure whose
life would symbolize the strengthened power of women. She
found Sacagawea (or Sacajawea) buried in the journals of
Lewis and Clark. The Shoshoni teenager had traveled with
the Lewis and Clark expedition, carrying her infant son, and
on a small number of occasions acted as translator.[6]
Dye declared that Sacagawea, whose name is thought to

mean Bird Woman, had been the guide to the historic expedition, and through Dye's work Sacagawea became enshrined in American memory as a moving force and friend of the whites, leading them in the settlement of western North America.[7]

But Native American roots of white feminism reach back beyond Sacagawea. The earliest white women on this continent were well acquainted with tribal women. They were neighbors to a number of tribes and often shared food, information, child care, and health care. Of course little is made of these encounters in official histories of colonial America, the period from the Revolution to the Civil War, or on the ever-moving frontier. Nor, to my knowledge, has either the significance or incidence of intermarriage between Indian and white or between Indian and Black been explored. By and large, the study of Indian-white relations has been focused on government and treaty relations, warfare, missionization, and education. It has been almost entirely documented in terms of formal white Christian patriarchal impacts and assaults on Native Americans, though they are not often characterized as assaults but as "civilizing the savages." Particularly in organs of popular culture and miseducation, the focus has been on what whites imagine to be degradation of Indian women ("squaws"), their equally imagined love of white government and white conquest ("princesses"), and the horrifyingly misleading, fanciful tales of "bloodthirsty, backward primitives" assaulting white Christian settlers who were looking for life, liberty, and happiness in their chosen land.

But, regardless of official versions of relations between Indians and whites or other segments of the American population, the fact remains that great numbers of apparently "white" or "Black" Americans carry notable degrees of Indian blood. With that blood has come the culture of the Indians, informing the lifestyles, attitudes, and values of their descendants. Somewhere along the line – and often quite recently – an Indian woman was giving birth to and raising the children of a family both officially and informally designated as white or Black – not Indian. In view of this, it should be evident that one of the major enterprises of Indian women in America has been the transfer of Indian values and culture to as large and influential a segment of American immigrant populations as possible. Their success in this endeavor is amply demonstrated in the Indian values and social styles that increasingly characterize American life. Among these must be included "permissive" childrearing practices, for imprisoning, torturing, caning, strapping, starving, or verbally abusing children was considered outrageous behavior. Native Americans did not believe that physical or psychological abuse of children would result in their edification. They did not believe that children are born in sin, are congenitally predisposed to evil, or that a good parent who wishes the child to gain salvation, achieve success, or earn the respect of her or his fellows can be helped to those ends by physical or emotional torture.

The early Americans saw the strongly protective attitude of the Indian people as a mark of their "savagery" – as they saw the Indian's habit of bathing frequently, their sexual openness, their liking for scant clothing, their raucous laughter at most things, their suspicion and derision of authoritarian structures, their quick pride, their genuine courtesy, their willingness to share what they had with others less fortunate than they, their egalitarianism, their ability to act as if various lifestyles were a normal part of living, and their granting that women were of equal or, in individual cases, of greater value than men.

Yet the very qualities that marked Indian life in the sixteenth century have, over the centuries since contact between the two worlds occurred, come to mark much of contemporary American life. And those qualities, which I believe have passed into white culture from Indian culture, are the very ones that fundamentalists, immigrants from Europe, the Middle East, and Asia often find the most reprehensible. Third- and fourth-generation Americans indulge in growing nudity, informality in social relations, egalitarianism, and the rearing of women who value autonomy, strength, freedom, and personal dignity – and who are often derided by European, Asian, and

Middle Eastern men for those qualities. Contemporary Americans value leisure almost as much as tribal people do. They find themselves increasingly unable to accept child abuse as a reasonable way to nurture. They bathe more than any other industrial people on earth – much to the scorn of their white cousins across the Atlantic, and they sometimes enjoy a good laugh even at their own expense (though they still have a less developed sense of the ridiculous than one might wish).

Contemporary Americans find themselves more and more likely to adopt a "live and let live" attitude in matters of personal sexual and social styles. Two-thirds of their diet and a large share of their medications and medical treatments mirror or are directly derived from Native American sources. Indianization is not a simple concept, to be sure, and it is one that Americans often find themselves resisting; but it is a process that has taken place, regardless of American resistance to recognizing the source of many if not most of American's vaunted freedoms in our personal, family, social, and political arenas.

This is not to say that Americans have become Indian in every attitude, value, or social institution. Unfortunately, Americans have a way to go in learning how to live in the world in ways that improve the quality of life for each individual while doing minimal damage to the biota, but they have adapted certain basic qualities of perception and certain attitudes that are moving them in that direction.

An Indian-Focused Version of American History

American colonial ideas of self-government came as much from the colonists' observations of tribal governments as from their Protestant or Greco-Roman heritage. Neither Greece nor Rome had the kind of pluralistic democracy as that concept has been understood in the United States since Andrew Jackson, but the tribes, particularly the gynarchical tribal confederacies, did. It is true that the *oligarchic* form of government that colonial Americans established was originally based on Greco-Roman systems in a number of important ways, such as its restriction of citizenship to propertied white males over twenty-one years of age, but it was never a form that Americans as a whole have been entirely comfortable with. Politics and government in the United States during the Federalist period also reflected the English common-law system as it had evolved under patriarchal feudalism and monarchy – hence the United States' retention of slavery and restriction of citizenship to propertied white males.

The Federalists did make one notable change in the feudal system from which their political system derived on its Anglo side. They rejected blooded aristocracy and monarchy. This idea came from the Protestant Revolt to be sure, but it was at least reinforced by colonial America's proximity to American Indian nonfeudal confederacies and their concourse with those confederacies over the two hundred years of the colonial era. It was this proximity and concourse that enabled the revolutionary theorists to "dream up" a system in which all local polities would contribute to and be protected by a central governing body responsible for implementing policies that bore on the common interest of all. It should also be noted that the Reformation followed Columbus's contact with the Americas and that his and Martyr's reports concerning Native Americans' free and easy egalitarianism were in circulation by the time the Reformation took hold.

The Iroquois federal system, like that of several in the vicinity of the American colonies, is remarkably similar to the organization of the federal system of the United States. It was made up of local, "state," and federal bodies composed of executive, legislative, and judicial branches. The Council of Matrons was the executive: it instituted and determined general policy. The village, tribal (several villages), and Confederate councils determined and implemented policies when they did not conflict with the broader Council's decisions or with theological precepts that ultimately determined policy at all levels. The judicial was composed of the men's councils and the Matron's council, who sat together to make decisions. Because the matrons were the ceremonial center of the system, they were also the prime policymakers.

Obviously, there are major differences between the structure of the contemporary American government and that of the Iroquois. Two of those differences were and are crucial to the process of just government. The Iroquois system is spirit-based, while that of the United States is secular, and the Iroquois Clan Matrons formed the executive. The female executive function was directly tied to the ritual nature of the Iroquois politic, for the executive was lodged in the hands of the Matrons of particular clans across village, tribe, and national lines. The executive office was hereditary, and only sons of eligible clans could serve, at the behest of the Matrons of their clans, on the councils at the three levels. Certain daughters inherited the office of Clan Matron through their clan affiliations. No one could impeach or disempower a Matron, though her violation of certain laws could result in her ineligibility for the Matron's council. For example, a woman who married *and took her husband's name* could not hold the title Matron.

American ideals of social justice came into sharp focus through the commentaries of Iroquois observers who traveled in France in the colonial period. These observers expressed horror at the great gap between the lifestyles of the wealthy and the poor, remarking to the French philosopher Montaigne, who would heavily influence the radical communities of Europe, England, and America, that "they had noticed that in Europe there seemed to be two moities, consisting of the rich 'full gorged' with wealth, and the poor, starving 'and bare with need and povertie.' The Indian tourists not only marveled at the division, but marveled that the poor endured 'such an injustice, and that they took not the others by the throte, or set fire on their house.' "[8] It must be noted that the urban poor eventually did just that in the French Revolution. The writings of Montaigne and of those he influenced provided the theoretical framework and the vision that propelled the struggle for liberty, justice, and equality on the Continent and later throughout the British empire.

The feminist idea of power as it ideally accrues to women stems from tribal sources. The central importance of the clan Matrons in the formulation and determination of domestic and foreign policy as well as in their primary role in the ritual and ceremonial life of their respective Nations was the single most important attribute of the Iroquois, as of the Cherokee and Muskogee, who traditionally inhabited the southern Atlantic region. The latter peoples were removed to what is now Oklahoma during the Jackson administration, but prior to the American Revolution they had regular and frequent communication with and impact on both the British colonizers and later the American people, including the African peoples brought here as slaves.

Ethnographer Lewis Henry Morgan wrote an account of Iroquoian matriarchal culture, published in 1877,[9] that heavily influenced Marx and the development of communism, particularly lending it the idea of the liberation of women from patriarchal dominance. The early socialists in Europe, especially in Russia, saw women's liberation as a central aspect of the socialist revolution. Indeed, the basic ideas of socialism, the egalitarian distribution of goods and power, the peaceful ordering of society, and the right of every member of society to participate in the work and benefits of that society, are ideas that pervade American Indian political thought and action. And it is through various channels – the informal but deeply effective Indianization of Europeans, and christianizing Africans, the social and political theory of the confederacies feuding and then intertwining with European dreams of liberty and justice, and, more recently, the work of Morgan and the writings of Marx and Engels – that the age-old gynarchical systems of egalitarian government found their way into contemporary feminist theory.

When Eva Emery Dye discovered Sacagawea and honored her as the guiding spirit of American womanhood, she may have been wrong in bare historical fact, but she was quite accurate in terms of deeper truth. The statues that have been erected depicting Sacagawea as a Matron in her prime signify an understanding in the American mind, however unconscious, that the source of just government, of right ordering of social relationships, the dream of "liberty and justice for all" can be gained only by following the Indian Matrons' guidance. For, as Dr. Anna Howard Shaw said of Sacagawea at the National American Woman's Suffrage Association in 1905:

> Forerunner of civilization, great leader of men, patient and motherly woman, we bow our hearts to do you honor! . . . May we the daughters of an alien race . . . learn the lessons of calm endurance, of patient persistence and unfaltering courage exemplified in your life, in our efforts to lead men through the Pass of justice, which goes over the mountains of prejudice and conservatism to the broad land of the perfect freedom of a true republic; one in which men and women together shall in perfect equality solve the problems of a nation that knows no caste, no race, no sex in opportunity, in responsibility or in justice! May 'the eternal womanly' ever lead us on! [10]

GLORIA ANZALDÚA

Tlilli, Tlapalli:
The Path of the Red and Black Ink

"Out of poverty, poetry;
out of suffering, song."

– *a Mexican saying*

When I was seven, eight, nine, fifteen, sixteen years old, I would read in bed with a flashlight under the covers, hiding my self-imposed insomnia from my mother. I preferred the world of the imagination to the death of sleep. My sister, Hilda, who slept in the same bed with me, would threaten to tell my mother unless I told her a story.

I was familiar with *cuentos* – my grandmother told stories like the one about her getting on top of the roof while down below rabid coyotes were ravaging the place and wanting to get at her. My father told stories about a phantom giant dog that appeared out of nowhere and sped along the side of the pickup no matter how fast he was driving.

Nudge a Mexican and she or he will break out with a story. So, huddling under the covers, I made up stories for my sister night after night. After a while she wanted two stories per night. I learned to give her installments, building up the suspense with convoluted complications until the story climaxed several nights later. It must have been then that I decided to put stories on paper. It must have been then that working with images and writing became connected to night.

Invoking Art

In the ethno-poetics and performance of the shaman, my people, the Indians, did not split the artistic from the functional, the sacred from the secular, art from everyday life. The religious, social, and aesthetic purposes of art were all intertwined. Before the Conquest, poets gathered to play music, dance, sing, and read poetry in open-air places around the *Xochicuahuitl, el Arbol Florido,* Tree-in-Flower. (The *Coaxihuitl* or morning glory is called the snake plant and its seeds, known as *ololiuhqui,* are hallucinogenic.[1]) The ability of story (prose and poetry) to transform the storyteller and the listener into something or someone else is shamanistic. The writer, as shape-changer, is a *nahual,* a shaman.

In looking over the book from which this essay was taken, I see a mosaic pattern (Aztec-like) emerging, a weaving pattern, thin here, thick there. I see a preoccupation with the deep structure, the underlying structure, with the gesso underpainting that is red earth, black earth. I can see the deep structure, the scaffolding. If I can get the bone structure right, then putting flesh on it proceeds without too many hitches. The problem is that the bones often do not exist prior to the flesh, but are shaped after a vague and broad shadow of its form is discerned or uncovered during beginning, middle, and final stages of the writing. Numerous overlays of paint, rough surfaces, smooth surfaces make me realize I am preoccupied with texture as well. Too, I see the barely contained color threatening to spill over the boundaries of the object it represents and into other "objects" and over the borders of the frame. I see a hybridization of metaphor, different species of ideas popping up here, popping up there, full of variations and seeming contradictions, though I believe in an ordered, structured universe where all phenomena are interrelated and imbued with spirit. This book seems an assemblage, a montage, a beaded work with several leitmotifs and with a central core, now appearing, now disappearing in a crazy dance. The whole thing has had a mind of its own, escaping me and insisting on putting together the pieces of its own puzzle with minimal direction from my will. It is a rebellious, willful entity, a precocious girl-child forced to grow up too quickly, rough, unyielding, with pieces of feather sticking out here and there, fur, twigs, clay. My child, but not for much longer. This female being is angry, sad, joyful, is *Coatlicue*, dove, horse, serpent, cactus. Though it is a flawed thing – a clumsy, complex, groping blind thing – for me it is alive, infused with spirit. I talk to it; it talks to me.

I make my offerings of incense and cracked corn, light my candle. In my head I sometimes will say a prayer – an affirmation and a voicing of intent. Then I run water, wash the dishes or my underthings, take a bath, or mop the kitchen floor. This "induction" period sometimes takes a few minutes, sometimes hours. But always I go against a resistance. Something in me does not want to do this writing. Yet once I'm immersed in it, I can go fifteen to seventeen hours in one sitting and I don't want to leave it.

My "stories" are acts encapsulated in time, "enacted" every time they are spoken aloud or read silently. I like to think of them as performances and not as inert and "dead" objects (as the aesthetics of Western culture think of art works). Instead, the work has an identity; it is a "who" or a "what" and contains the presences of persons, that is, incarnations of gods or ancestors or natural and cosmic powers. The work manifests the same needs as a person, it needs to be "fed," *la tengo que bañar y vestir.*

When invoked in rite, the object/event is "present"; that is, "enacted," it is both a physical thing and the power that infuses it. It is metaphysical in that it "spins its energies between gods and humans" and its task is to move the gods. This type of work dedicates itself to managing the universe and its energies. I'm not sure what it is when it is at rest (not in performance). It may or may not be a "work" then. A mask may only have the power of presence during a ritual dance and the rest of the time is may merely be a "thing." Some works exist forever invoked, always in performance. I'm thinking of totem poles, cave paintings. Invoked art is communal and speaks of everyday life. It is dedicated to the validation of humans; that is, it makes people hopeful, happy, secure, and it can have negative effects as well, which propel one towards a search for validation.[2]

The aesthetic of virtuosity, art typical of Western European cultures, attempts to manage the energies of its own internal system such as conflicts, harmonies, resolutions and balances. It bears the presences of qualities and internal meanings. It is dedicated to the validation of itself. Its task is to move humans by means of achieving mastery in content, technique, feeling. Western art is always whole and always "in power." It is individual (not communal). It is "psychological" in that it spins its energies between itself and its witness.[3]

Western cultures behave differently toward works of art than do tribal cultures. The "sacrifices" Western cultures make are in housing their art works in the best structures designed by the best architects; and in servicing them with insurance, guards to protect them, conservators to maintain them, specialists to mount and display them, and the educated and upper classes to "view" them. Tribal cultures keep art works in honored and sacred places in the home and elsewhere. They attend them by making sacrifices of blood (goat or chicken), libations of wine. They bathe, feed, and clothe them. The works are treated not just as objects, but also as persons. The "witness" is a participant in the enactment of the work in a ritual, and not a member of the privileged classes.[4]

Ethnocentrism is the tyranny of Western aesthetics. An Indian mask in an American museum is transported into an alien aesthetic system where what is missing is the presence of power invoked through performance ritual. It has become a conquered thing, a dead "thing" separated from nature and, therefore, its power.

Modern Western painters have "borrowed," copied, or otherwise extrapolated the art of tribal cultures and called it cubism, surrealism, symbolism. The music, the beat of the drum, the Blacks' jive talk. All taken over. Whites, along with a good number of our own people, have cut themselves off from their spiritual roots, and they take our spiritual art objects in an unconscious attempt to get them back. If they're going to do it, I'd like them to be aware of what they are doing and to go about doing it the right way. Let's all stop importing Greek myths and the Western Cartesian split point of view and root ourselves in the mythological soil and soul of this continent. White America has only attended to the body of the earth in order to exploit it, never to succor it or to be nurtured in it. Instead of surreptitiously ripping off the vital energy of people of color and putting it to commercial use, whites could allow themselves to share and exchange and learn from us in a respectful way. By taking up *curanderismo,* Santeria, shamanism, Taoism, Zen, and otherwise delving into the spiritual life and ceremonies of multi-colored people, Anglos would perhaps lose the white sterility they have in their kitchens, bathrooms, hospitals, mortuaries, and missile bases. Though in the conscious mind, black and dark may be associated with death, evil, and destruction, in the subconscious mind and in our dreams, white is associated with disease, death, and hopelessness. Let us hope that the left hand, that of darkness, of femaleness, of "primitiveness," can divert the indifferent, right-handed, "rational" suicidal drive that, unchecked, could blow us into acid rain in a fraction of a millisecond.

Ni cuicani: I, the Singer

For the ancient Aztecs, *tlilli, tlapalli, la tinta negra y roja de sus códices* (the black and red ink painted on codices) were the colors symbolizing *escritura y sabiduría* (writing and wisdom).[5] They believed that through metaphor and symbol, by means of poetry and truth, communication with the Divine could be attained, and *topan* (that which is above – the gods and spirit world) could be bridged with *mictlán* (that which is below – the underworld and the region of the dead).

> Poet: she pours water from the mouth of the pump, lowers the handle then lifts it, lowers, lifts. Her hands begin to feel the pull from the entrails, the live animal resisting. A sigh rises up from the depths, the handle becomes a wild thing in her hands, the cold sweet water gushes out, splashing her face, the shock of nightlight filling the bucket.

An image is a bridge between evoked emotion and conscious knowledge; words are the cables that hold up the bridge. Images are more direct, more immediate than words, and closer to the unconscious. Picture language precedes thinking in words; the metaphorical mind precedes analytical consciousness.

The Shamanic State

When I create stories in my head, that is, allow the voices and scenes to be projected in the inner screen of my mind, I "trance." I used to think I was going crazy or that I was having hallucinations. But now I realize it is my job, my calling, to traffic in images. Some of these film-like narratives I write down; most are lost, forgotten. When I don't write the images down for several days or weeks or months, I get physically ill. Because writing invokes images from my unconscious, and because some of the images are residues of trauma which I then have to reconstruct, I sometimes get sick when I *do* write. I can't stomach it, become nauseous, or burn with fever, worsen. But, in reconstructing the traumas behind the images, I make "sense" of them, and once they have "meaning" they are changed, transformed. It is then that writing heals me, brings me great joy.

To facilitate the "movies" with soundtracks, I need to be alone, or in a sensory-deprived state. I plug up my ears with wax, put on my black cloth eye-shades, lie horizontal and unmoving, in a state between sleeping and waking, mind and body locked into my fantasy. I am held prisoner by it. My body is experiencing events. In the beginning it is like being in a movie theater, as pure spectator. Gradually I become so engrossed with the activities, the conversations, that I become a participant in the drama. I have to struggle to "disengage" or escape from my "animated story," I have to get some sleep so I can write tomorrow. Yet I am gripped by a story which won't let me go. Outside the frame, I am film director, screenwriter, camera operator. Inside the frame, I am the actors – male and female – I am desert sand, mountain, I am dog, mosquito. I can sustain a four- to six-hour "movie." Once I am up, I can sustain several "shorts" of anywhere between five and thirty minutes. Usually these "narratives" are the offspring of stories acted out in my head during periods of sensory deprivation.

My "awakened dreams" are about shifts. Thought shifts, reality shifts, gender shifts: one person metamorphoses into another in a world where people fly through the air, heal from mortal wounds. I am playing with my Self, I am playing with the world's soul, I am the dialogue between my Self and *el espíritu del mundo*. I change myself, I change the world.

Sometimes I put the imagination to a more rare use. I choose words, images, and body sensations and animate them to impress them on my consciousness, thereby making changes in my belief system and reprogramming my consciousness. This involves looking my inner demons in the face, then deciding which I want in my psyche. Those I don't want, I starve; I feed them no words, no images, no feelings. I spend no time with them, share not my home with them. Neglected, they leave. This is harder to do than to merely generate "stories." I can only sustain this activity for a few minutes.

I write the myths in me, the myths I am, the myths I want to become. The word, the image and the feeling have a palatable energy, a kind of power. *Con imagenes domo mi miedo, cruzo los abismos que tengo por dentro. Con palabras me hago piedra, pájaro, puente de serpientes arrastrando a ras del suelo todo lo que soy, todo lo que algún día seré.*

> *Los que están mirando (leyendo),*
> *los que cuentan (o refieran lo que leen).*
> *Los que vuelven ruidosamente las hojas de los códices.*
> *Los que tienen en su poder*
> *la tinta negra y roja (la sabiduría)*
> *y lo pintado,*
> *ellos nos llevan, nos guían,*
> *nos dicen el camino.*[6]

Writing Is a Sensuous Act

Tallo mi cuerpo como si estuviera lavando un trapo. Toco las saltadas venas de mis manos, mis chichis adormecidas como pájaras a la anochecer. Estoy encorbada sobre la cama. Las imagenes aleteán alrededor de mi cama como murciélagos, la sábana como que tuviese alas. El ruido de los trenes subterráneos en mi sentido como conchas. Parece que las paredes del cuarto se me arriman cada vez más cerquita.

Picking out images from my soul's eye, fishing for the right words to recreate the images. Words are blades of grass pushing past the obstacles, sprouting on the page; the spirit of the words moving in the body is as concrete as flesh and as palpable; the hunger to create is as substantial as fingers and hand.

I look at my fingers, see plumes growing there. From the fingers, my feathers, black and red ink drips across the page. *Escribo con la tinta de mi sangre.* I write in red. Intimately knowing the smooth touch of paper, its speechlessness before I spill myself on the insides of trees. Daily, I battle the silence and the red. Daily, I take my throat in my hands and squeeze until the cries pour out, my larynx and soul sore from the constant struggle.

Something to Do with the Dark

"Quien canta, sus males espanta."
– un dicho

The toad comes out of its hiding place inside the lobes of my brain. It's going to happen again. The ghost of the toad that betrayed me – I hold it in my hand. The toad is sipping the strength from my veins, it is sucking my pale heart. I am a dried serpent skin, wind scuttling me across the hard ground, pieces of me scattered over the countryside. And there in the dark I meet the crippled spider crawling in the gutter, the day-old newspaper fluttering in the dirty rain water.

> *Musa bruja, venga. Cubrese con una sábana y espante mis demonios que a rempujones y a cachetadas me roban la pluma me rompen el sueño. Musa, ¡misericordia!*
>
> *Óigame, musa bruja. ¿Porqué huye uste' en mi cara? Su grito me desarrolla de mi caracola, me sacude el alma. Vieja, quítese de aquí con sus alas de navaja. Ya no me despedaze mi cara. Vaya con sus pinche uñas que me desgarran de los ojos hasta los talones. Váyase a la tiznada. Que no me coman, le digo. Que no me coman sus nueve dedos caníbales.*
>
> *Hija negra de la noche, carnala, ¿Porqué me sacas las tripas, porqué cardas mis entrañas? Este hilvanando palabras con tripas me está matando. Jija de la noche ¡vete a la chingada!*

Writing produces anxiety. Looking inside myself and my experience, looking at my conflicts, engenders anxiety in me. Being a writer feels very much like being a Chicana, or being queer – a lot of squirming, coming up against all sorts of walls. Or its opposite: nothing defined or definite, a boundless, floating state of limbo where I kick my heels, brood, percolate, hibernate, and wait for something to happen.

Living in a state of psychic unrest, in a Borderland, is what makes poets write and artists create. It is like a cactus needle embedded in the flesh. It worries itself deeper and deeper, and I keep aggravating it by poking at it. When it begins to fester I have to do something to put an end to the aggravation and to figure out why I have it. I get deep down into the place where it's rooted in my skin and pluck away at it, playing it like a musical instrument – the fingers pressing, making the pain worse before it can get better. Then out it comes. No more discomfort, no more ambivalence. Until another needle pierces the skin. That's what writing is for me, an endless cycle of making it worse, making it better, but always making meaning out of the experience, whatever it may be.

> My flowers shall not cease to live;
> my songs shall never end:
> I, a singer, intone them;
> they become scattered, they are spread about.
> – *Cantares mexicanos*

To write, to be a writer, I have to trust and believe in myself as a speaker, as a voice for the images. I have to believe that I can communicate with images and words and that I can do it well. A lack of belief in my creative self is a lack of belief in my total self and vice versa – I cannot separate my writing from any part of my life. It is all one.

When I write it feels like I'm carving bone. It feels like I'm creating my own face, my own heart – a Nahuatl concept. My soul makes itself through the creative act. It is constantly re-making and giving birth to itself through my body. It is this learning to live with *la Coatlicue* that transforms living in the Borderlands from a nightmare into a numinous experience. It is always a path/state to something else.

In *Xóchitl* in *Cuícatl* [7]

She writes while other people sleep. Something is trying to come out. She fights the words, pushes them down, down, a woman with morning sickness in the middle of the night. How much easier it would be to carry a baby for nine months and

then expel it permanently. These continuous multiple preg-
nancies are going to kill her. She is the battlefield for the
pitched fight between the inner image and the words trying to
recreate it. *La musa bruja* has no manners. Doesn't she know,
nights are for sleeping?

She is getting too close to the mouth of the abyss. She is
teetering on the edge, trying to balance while she makes up her
mind whether to jump in or find a safer way down. That's why
she makes herself sick – to postpone having to jump blind-
folded into the abyss of her own being and there in the depths
confront her face, the face underneath the mask.

To be a mouth – the cost is too high – her whole life enslaved
to that devouring mouth. *Todo pasaba por esa boca, el viento, el
fuego, los mares y la Tierra.* Her body, a crossroads, a fragile
bridge, cannot support the tons of cargo passing through it.
She wants to install 'stop' and 'go' signal lights, instigate a cur-
few, police Poetry. But something wants to come out.

Blocks (*Coatlicue* states) are related to my cultural identity.
The painful periods of confusion that I suffer from are symp-
tomatic of a larger creative process: cultural shifts. The stress
of living with cultural ambiguity both compels me to write
and blocks me. It isn't until I'm almost at the end of the
blocked state that I remember and recognize it for what it is.
As soon as this happens, the piercing light of awareness melts
the block and I accept the deep and the darkness and I hear
one of my voices saying, "I am tired of fighting. I surrender. I
give up, let go, let the walls fall. On this night of the hearing
of faults, *Tlazolteotl, diosa de la cara negra*, let fall the cock
roaches that live in my hair, the rats that nestle in my skull.
Gouge out my lame eyes, rout my demon from its nocturnal
cave. Set torch to the tiger that stalks me. Loosen the dead
faces gnawing at my cheekbones. I am tired of resisting. I
surrender. I give up, let go, let the walls fall."

And in descending to the depths I realize that down is up,
and I rise up from and into the deep. And once again I
recognize that the internal tension of oppositions can propel

(if it doesn't tear apart) the mestiza writer out of the *metate* where she is being ground with corn and water, eject her out as *nahual,* an agent of transformation, able to modify and shape primordial energy and therefore able to change herself and others into turkey, coyote, tree, or human.

I sit here before my computer, *Amiguita,* my altar on top of the monitor with the *Virgen de Coatlalopeuh* candle and copal incense burning. My companion, a wooden serpent staff with feathers, is to my right while I ponder the ways metaphor and symbol concretize the spirit and etherealize the body. The Writing is my whole life, it is my obsession. This vampire which is my talent does not suffer other suitors.[9] Daily I court it, offer my neck to its teeth. This is the sacrifice that the act of creation requires, a blood sacrifice. For only through the body, through the pulling of flesh, can the human soul be transformed. And for images, words, stories to have this transformative power, they must arise from the human body – flesh and bone – and from the Earth's body – stone, sky, liquid, soil. This work, these images, piercing tongue or ear lobes with cactus needle, are my offerings, are my Aztecan blood sacrifices.

WENDELL BERRY

People, Land,

and Community

I would like to speak more precisely than I have before of the connections that join people, land, and community – to describe, for example, the best human use of a problematical hillside farm. In a healthy culture, these connections are complex. The industrial economy breaks them down by oversimplifying them and in the process raises obstacles that make it hard for us to see what the connections are or ought to be. These are mental obstacles, of course, and there appear to be two major ones: the assumption that knowledge (information) can be "sufficient," and the assumption that time and work are short.

These assumptions will be found implicit in a whole set of contemporary beliefs: that the future can be studied and planned for; that limited supplies can be wasted without harm; that good intentions can safeguard the use of nuclear power. A recent newspaper article says, for example, "A congressionally mandated study of the Ogallala Aquifer is finding no great cause for alarm from [sic] its rapidly dropping levels. The director of the . . . study . . . says that even at current rates of pumping, the aquifer can supply the Plains with water for another forty to fifty years. . . . All six states participating in the study . . . are forecasting increased farm yields based on improved technology." Another article speaks of a different technology with the same optimism: "The nation has invested hundreds of billions of dollars in atomic weapons and at the same time has developed the most sophisticated strategies to fine-tune their use to avoid a holocaust. Yet the system that is meant to activate them is the weakest link in the chain.... Thus, some have suggested that what may be needed are warning systems for the warning systems."

Always the assumption is that we can first set demons at large, and then, somehow, become smart enough to control them. This is not childishness. It is not even "human weakness." It is a kind of idiocy, but perhaps we will not cope with it and save ourselves until we regain the sense to call it evil.

The trouble, as in our conscious moments we all know, is that we are terrifyingly ignorant. The most learned of us are ignorant. The acquisition of knowledge always involves the revelation of ignorance – almost *is* the revelation of ignorance. Our knowledge of the world instructs us first of all that the world is greater than our knowledge of it. To those who rejoice in the abundance and intricacy of Creation, this is a source of joy, as it is to those who rejoice in freedom. ("The future comes only by surprise," we say, "– thank God!") To those would-be solvers of "the human problem," who hope for knowledge equal to (capable of controlling) the world, it is a source of unremitting defeat and bewilderment. The evidence is overwhelming that knowledge does not solve "the human problem." Indeed, the evidence overwhelmingly suggests – with Genesis – that knowledge *is* the problem. Or perhaps we should say instead that all our problems tend to gather under two questions about knowledge: Having the ability and desire to know, how and what should we learn? And, having learned, how and for what should we use what we know?

One thing we do know, that we dare not forget, is that better solutions than ours have at times been made by people with much less information than we have. We know too, from the study of agriculture, that the same information, tools, and techniques that in one farmer's hands will ruin land, in another's will save and improve it.

This is not a recommendation of ignorance. To know nothing, after all, is no more possible than to know enough. I am only proposing that knowledge, like everything else, has its place, and that we need urgently now to *put* it in its place. If we want to know and cannot help knowing, then let us learn as fully and accurately as we decently can. But let us at the same time abandon our superstitious beliefs about knowledge: that it is ever sufficient; that it can of itself solve problems; that it is intrinsically good; that it can be used objectively or disinterestedly. Let us acknowledge that the objective or disinterested researcher is always on the side that pays best. And let us give up our forlorn pursuit of the "informed decision."

The "informed decision," I suggest, is as fantastical a creature as the "disinterested third party" and the "objective observer." Or it is if by "informed" we mean "supported by sufficient information." A great deal of our public life, and certainly the most expensive part of it, rests on the assumed possibility of decisions so informed. Examination of private life, however, affords no comfort whatsoever to that assumption. It is simply true that we do not and cannot *know* enough to make any important decision.

Of this dilemma we can take marriage as an instance, for as a condition marriage reveals the insufficiency of knowledge, and as an institution it suggests the possibility that decisions can be informed in another way that *is* sufficient, or approximately so. I take it as an axiom that one cannot know enough to get married, any more than one can predict a surprise. The only people who possess information sufficient to their vows are widows and widowers – who do not know enough to *re*marry.

What is not so well understood now as perhaps it used to be is that marriage is made in an inescapable condition of loneliness and ignorance, to which it, or something like it, is the only possible answer. Perhaps this is so hard to understand now because now the most noted solutions are mechanical solutions, which are often exactly suited to mechanical problems. But we are humans – which means that we not only *have* problems but *are* problems. Marriage is not as nicely trimmed to its purpose as a bottle-stopper; it is a not entirely possible solution to a not entirely soluble problem. And this is true of the other human connections. We can commit ourselves fully to anything – a place, a discipline, a life's work, a child, a family, a community, a faith, a friend – only in the same poverty of knowledge, the same ignorance of result, the same self-subordination, the same final forsaking of other possibilities. If we must make these so final commitments without sufficient information, then what *can* inform our decisions?

In spite of the obvious dangers of the word, we must say first that love can inform them. This, of course, though probably necessary, is not safe. What parent, faced with a child who is in love and going to get married, has not been filled with mistrust and fear – and justly so. We who were lovers before we were parents know what a fraudulent justifier love can be. We know that people stay married for different reasons than those for which they get married and that the later reasons will have to be discovered. Which, of course, is not to say that the later reasons may not confirm the earlier ones; it is to say only that the earlier ones must wait for confirmation.

But our decisions can also be informed – our loves both limited and strengthened – by those patterns of value and restraint, principle and expectation, memory, familiarity, and understanding that, inwardly, add up to *character* and, outwardly, to *culture*. Because of these patterns, and only because of them, we are not alone in the bewilderments of the human condition and human love, but have the company and the comfort of the best of our kind, living and dead. These patterns constitute a knowledge far different from the kind I have been talking about. It is a kind of knowledge that includes information, but is never the same as information. Indeed, if we study the paramount documents of our culture, we will see that this second kind of knowledge invariably implies, and often explicitly imposes, limits upon the first kind: some possibilities must not be explored; some things must not be learned. If we want to get safely home, there are certain seductive songs we must not turn aside for, some sacred things we must not meddle with:

> Great captain,
> a fair wind and the honey lights of home
> are all you seek. But anguish lies ahead;
> the god who thunders on the land prepares it . . .
> . . . .
> One narrow strait may take you through his blows:
> denial of yourself, restraint of shipmates.

This theme, of course, is dominant in Biblical tradition, but the theme itself and its modern inversion can be handily understood by a comparison of this speech of Tirêsias to Odysseus in Robert Fitzgerald's Homer with Tennyson's romantic Ulysses who proposed, like a genetic engineer or an atomic scientist,

> To follow knowledge like a sinking star,
> Beyond the utmost bound of human thought.

Obviously unlike Homer's Odysseus, Tennyson's Ulysses is said to come from Dante, and he does resemble Dante's Ulysses pretty exactly – the critical difference being that Dante thought this Ulysses a madman and a fool, and brings down upon his Tennysonian speech to his sailors one of the swiftest anticlimaxes in literature. The real – the human – knowledge is understood as implying and imposing limits, much as marriage does, and these limits are understood to belong necessarily to the definition of a human being.

In all this talk about marriage I have not forgot that I am supposed to be talking about agriculture. I am going to talk directly about agriculture in a minute, but I want to insist that I have been talking about it indirectly all along, for the analogy between marriage making and farm making, marriage keeping and farm keeping, is nearly exact. I have talked about marriage as a way of talking about farming because marriage, as a human artifact, has been more carefully understood than farming. The analogy between them is so close, for one thing, because they join us to time in nearly the same way. In talking about time, I will begin to talk directly about farming, but as I do so, the reader will be aware, I hope, that I am talking indirectly about marriage.

When people speak with confidence of the longevity of diminishing agricultural sources – as when they speak of their good intentions about nuclear power – they are probably not just being gullible or thoughtless; they are likely to be speaking from belief in several tenets of industrial optimism: that life is long, but time and work are short; that every problem will be solved by a "technological breakthrough" before it enlarges to catastrophe; that *any* problem can be solved in a hurry by large applications of urgent emotion, information, and money. It is regrettable that these assumptions should risk correction by disaster when they could be cheaply and safely overturned by the study of any agriculture that has proved durable.

To the farmer, Emerson said, "The landscape is an armory of powers. . . ." As he meant it, the statement may be true, but the metaphor is ill-chosen, for the powers of a landscape are available to human use in nothing like so simple a way as are the powers of an armory. Or let us say, anyhow, that the preparations needed for the taking up of agricultural powers are more extensive and complex than those usually thought necessary for the taking up of arms. And let us add that the motives are, or ought to be, significantly different.

Arms are taken up in fear and hate, but it has not been uncharacteristic for a farmer's connection to a farm to begin in love. This has not always been so ignorant a love as it sometimes is now; but always, no matter what one's agricultural experience may have been, one's connection to a newly bought farm will begin in love that is more or less ignorant.

One loves the place because present appearances recommend it, and because they suggest possibilities irresistibly imaginable. One's head, like a lover's, grows full of visions. One walks over the premises, saying, "If this were mine, I'd make a permanent pasture here; here is where I'd plant an orchard; here is where I'd dig a pond." These visions are the usual stuff of unfulfilled love and induce wakefulness at night.

When one buys the farm and moves there to live, something different begins. Thoughts begin to be translated into acts. Truth begins to intrude with its matter-of-fact. One's work may be defined in part by one's visions, but it is defined in part too by problems, which the work leads to and reveals. And daily life, work, and problems gradually alter the visions. It invariably turns out, I think, that one's first vision of one's place was to some extent an imposition on it. But if one's sight is clear and if one stays on and works well, one's love gradually responds to the place as it really is, and one's visions gradually image possibilities that are really in it. Vision, possibility, work, and life – *all* have changed by mutual correction. Correct discipline, given enough time, gradually removes one's self from one's line of sight. One works to better purposes then and makes fewer mistakes, because at last one sees where one is. Two human possibilities of the highest order thus come within reach: what one wants can become the same as what one has, and one's knowledge can cause respect for what one knows.

"Correct discipline" and "enough time" are inseparable notions. Correct discipline cannot be hurried, for it is both the knowledge of what ought to be done, and the willingness to do it – *all* of it, properly. The good worker will not suppose that good work can be made properly answerable to haste, urgency, or even emergency. But the good worker knows too that after it is done work requires yet more time to prove its worth. One must stay to experience and study and understand the consequences – must understand them by living with them, and then correct them, if necessary, by longer living and more work. It won't do to correct mistakes made in one place by moving to another place, as has been the common fashion in America, or by adding on another place, as is the fashion in any sort of "growth economy." Seen this way, questions about farming become inseparable from questions about propriety of scale. A farm can be too big for a farmer to husband properly or pay proper attention to. Distraction is inimical to correct discipline, and enough time is beyond the reach of anyone who has too much to do. But we must go farther and see that propriety of scale is invariably associated with propriety of another kind: an understanding and acceptance of the human place in the order of Creation – a proper humility. There are some things the arrogant mind does not see; it is blinded by its vision of what it desires. It does not see what is already there; it never sees the forest that precedes the farm or the farm that precedes the shopping center; it will never understand that America was "discovered" by the Indians. It is the properly humbled mind in its proper place that sees truly, because – to give only one reason – it sees details.

And the good farmer understands that further limits are imposed upon haste by nature which, except for an occasional storm or earthquake, is in no hurry either. In the processes of most concern to agriculture – the building and preserving of fertility – nature is never in a hurry. During the last seventeen years, for example, I have been working at the restoration of a once exhausted hillside. Its scars are now healed over, though still visible, and this year it has provided abundant pasture, more than in any year since we have owned it. But to make it as good as it is now has taken seventeen years. If I had been a millionaire or if my family had been starving, it would still have taken seventeen years. It can be better than it now is, but that will take longer. For it to live fully in its own possibility, as it did before bad use ran it down, may take hundreds of years.

But to think of the human use of a piece of land as continuing through hundreds of years, we must greatly complicate our understanding of agriculture. Let us start a job of farming on a given place – say an initially fertile hillside in the Kentucky River Valley – and construe it through time:

1. To begin using this hillside for agricultural production – pasture or crop – is a matter of a year's work. This is work in the present tense, adequately comprehended by conscious intention and by the first sort of knowledge I talked about – information available to the farmer's memory and built into his methods, tools, and crop and livestock species. Understood in its present tense, the work does not reveal its value except insofar as the superficial marks of craftsmanship may be seen and judged. But excellent workmanship, as with a breaking plow, may prove as damaging as bad workmanship. The work has not revealed its connections to the place or to the worker. These connections are revealed in time.

2. To live on the hillside and use it for a lifetime gives the annual job of work a past and a future. To live on the hillside and use it without diminishing its fertility or wasting it by erosion still requires conscious intention and information, but now we must say *good* intention and *good* (that is, correct) information, resulting in *good* work. And to these we must now add *character*; the sort of knowledge that might properly be called familiarity, and the affections, habits, values, and virtues (conscious and unconscious) that would preserve good care and good work through hard times.

3. For human life to continue on the hillside through successive generations requires good use, good work, all along. For in any agricultural place that will waste or erode – and all will – bad work does not permit "muddling through"; sooner or later it ends human life. Human continuity is virtually synonymous with good farming, and good farming obviously must outlast the life of any good farmer. For it to do this, in addition to the preceding requirements, we must have *community*. Without community, the good work of a single farmer or a single family will not mean much or last long. For good farming to last, it must occur in a good farming community – that is, a neighborhood of people who know each other, who

understand their mutual dependences, and who place a proper value on good farming. In its cultural aspect, the community is an order of memories preserved consciously in instructions, songs, and stories, and both consciously and unconsciously in *ways*. A healthy culture holds preserving knowledge *in place* for a *long* time. That is, the essential wisdom accumulates in the community much as fertility builds in the soil. In both, death becomes potentiality.

People are joined to the land by work. Land, work, people, and community are all comprehended in the idea of culture. These connections cannot be understood or described by information – so many resources to be transformed by so many workers into so many products for so many consumers – because they are not quantitative. We can understand them only after we acknowledge that they should be harmonious – that a culture must be either shapely and saving or shapeless and destructive. To presume to describe land, work, people, and community by information, by quantities, seems invariably to throw them into competition with one another. Work is then understood to exploit the land, the people to exploit their work, the community to exploit its people. And then instead of land, work, people, and community, we have the industrial categories of resources, labor, management, consumers, and government. We have exchanged harmony for an interminable fuss, and the work of culture for the timed and harried labor of an industrial economy.

But let me bring these notions to the trial of a more particular example.

Wes Jackson and Marty Bender of the Land Institute have recently worked out a comparison between the energy economy of a farm using draft horses for most of its field work and that of an identical farm using tractors. This is a project a generation overdue, of the greatest interest and importance – in short, necessary. And the results will be shocking to those who assume a direct proportion between fossil fuel combustion and human happiness.

These results, however, have not fully explained one fact that Jackson and Bender had before them at the start of their analysis and that was still running ahead of them at the end: that in the last twenty-five or thirty years, the Old Order Amish, who use horses for farmwork, doubled their population and stayed in farming, whereas in the same period millions of mechanized farmers were driven out. The reason that this is not adequately explained by analysis of the two energy economies, I believe, is that the problem is by its nature beyond the reach of analysis of any kind. The real or whole reason must be impossibly complicated, having to do with nature, culture, religion, family and community life, as well as with agricultural methodology and economics. What I think we are up against is an unresolvable difference between thought and action, thought and life.

What works *poorly* in agriculture – monoculture, for instance, or annual accounting – can be pretty fully explained, because what works poorly is invariably some oversimplifying *thought* that subjugates nature, people, and culture. What works well ultimately defies explanation because it involves an order which in both magnitude and complexity is ultimately incomprehensible.

Here, then, is a prime example of the futility of a dependence on informaton. We cannot contain what contains us or comprehend what comprehends us. Yeats said that "Man can embody truth but he cannot know it." The part, that is, cannot comprehend the whole, though it can stand for it (and by it). Synecdoche is possible, and its possibility implies the possibility of harmony between part and whole. If we cannot work on the basis of sufficient information, then we have to work on the basis of an understanding of harmony. That, I take it, is what Sir Albert Howard and Wes Jackson mean when they tell us that we must study and emulate on our farms the natural integrities that precede and support agriculture.

The study of Amish agriculture, like the study of *any* durable agriculture, suggests that we live in sequences of patterns that are formally analogous. These sequences are probably hierarchical, at least in the sense that some patterns are more comprehensive than others; they tend to arrange themselves like internesting bowls – though any attempt to represent their order visually will oversimplify it.

And so we must suspect that Amish horse-powered farms work well, not because – or not *just* because – horses are energy-efficient, but because they are living creatures, and therefore fit harmoniously into a pattern of relationships that are necessarily biological, and that rhyme analogically from ecosystem to crop, from field to farmer. In other words, ecosystem, farm, field, crop, horse, farmer, family, and community are in certain critical ways *like* each other. They are, for instance, all related to health and fertility or reproductivity in about the same way. The health and fertility of each involves and is involved in the health and fertility of all.

It goes without saying that tools can be introduced into this agricultural and ecological order without jeopardizing it – but only up to a certain kind, scale, and power. To introduce a tractor into it, as the historical record now seems virtually to prove, is to begin its destruction. The tractor has been so destructive, I think, because it is *unlike* anything else in the agricultural order, and so it breaks the essential harmony. And with the tractor comes dependence on an energy supply that lies not only off the farm but outside agriculture and outside biological cycles and integrities. With the tractor, both farm and farmer become "resources" of the industrial economy, which always exploits its resources.

We would be wrong, of course, to say that anyone who farms with a tractor is a bad farmer. That is not true. What we must say, however, is that once a tractor is introduced into the pattern of a farm, certain necessary restraints and practices, once implicit in technology, must now reside in the character and consciousness of the farmer – at the same time that the economic pressure to cast off restraint and good practice has been greatly increased.

In a society addicted to facts and figures, anyone trying to speak for agricultural *harmony* is inviting trouble. The first

trouble is in trying to say what harmony is. It cannot be reduced to facts and figures – though the lack of it can. It is not
very visibly a function. Perhaps we can only say what it may be
like. It may, for instance, be like sympathetic vibration: "The
A string of a violin . . . is designed to vibrate most readily at
about 440 vibrations per second: the note A. If that same
note is played loudly not on the violin but near it, the violin A
string may hum in sympathy." This may have a practical ex-
emplification in the craft of the mud daubers which, as they
trowel mud into their nest walls, hum to it, or at it, communi-
cating a vibration that makes it easier to work, thus mastering
their material by a kind of song. Perhaps the hum of the mud
dauber only activates that anciently perceived likeness between all creatures and the earth of which they are made. For
as common wisdom holds, like *speaks to* like. And harmony
always involves such specificities of form as in the mud dauber's song and its nest, whereas information accumulates indis-
criminately, like noise.

Of course, in the order of creatures, humanity is a special
case. Humans, unlike mud daubers, are not naturally involved
in harmony. For humans, harmony is always a human product, an artifact, and if they do not know how to make it and
choose to make it, then they do not have it. And so I suggest
that, for humans, the harmony I am talking about may bear
an inescapable likeness to what we know as moral law – or
that, for humans, moral law is a significant part of the nota-
tion of ecological and agricultural harmony. A great many
people seem to have voted for information as a safe substitute
for virtue, but this ignores – among much else – the need to
prepare humans to live short lives in the face of long work
and long time.

Perhaps it is only when we focus our minds on our machines that time seems short. Time is always running out for
machines. They shorten our work, in a sense popularly approved, by simplifying it and speeding it up, but our work
perishes quickly in them too as they wear out and are dis-
carded. For the living Creation, on the other hand, time is

always coming. It is running out for the farm built on the industrial pattern; the industrial farm burns fertility as it burns fuel. For the farm built into the pattern of living things, as an analogue of forest or prairie, time is a bringer of gifts. These gifts may be welcomed and cared for. To some extent they may be expected. Only within strict limits are they the result of human intention and knowledge. They cannot in the usual sense be made. Only in the short term of industrial accounting can they be thought simply earnable. Over the real length of human time, to be earned they must be deserved.

From this rather wandering excursion I arrive at two conclusions.

The first is that the modern stereotype of an intelligent person is probably wrong. The prototypical modern intelligence seems to be that of the Quiz Kid – a human shape barely discernable in fluff of facts. It is understood that everything must be justified by facts, and facts are offered in justification of *everything*. If it is a fact that soil erosion is now a critical problem in American agriculture, then more facts will indicate that it is not as bad as it *could* be and that Iowa will continue to have topsoil for as long as seventy more years. If facts show that some people are undernourished in America, further facts reveal that we should all be glad we do not live in India. This, of course, is machine thought.

To think better, to think like the best of humans, we are probably going to have to learn again to judge a person's intelligence, not by the ability to recite facts, but by the good order or harmoniousness of his or her surroundings. We must suspect that any statistical justification of ugliness and violence is a revelation of stupidity. As an earlier student of agriculture put it: "The intelligent man, however unlearned, may be known by his surroundings, and by the care of his horse, if he is fortunate enough to own one."

My second conclusion is that any public program to preserve

land or produce food is hopeless if it does not tend to right the balance between numbers of people and acres of land, and to encourage long-term, stable connections between families and small farms. It could be argued that our nation has never made an effort in this direction that was knowledgeable enough or serious enough. It is certain that no such effort, here, has ever succeeded. The typical American farm is probably sold and remade – often as part of a larger farm – at least every generation. Farms that have been passed to the second generation of the same family are unusual. Farms that have passed to the third generation are rare.

But our crying need is for an agriculture in which the typical farm would be farmed by the third generation of the same family. It would be wrong to try to say exactly what kind of agriculture that would be, but it may be allowable to suggest that certain good possibilities would be enhanced.

The most important of those possibilities would be the lengthening of memory. Previous mistakes, failures, and successes would be remembered. The land would not have to pay the cost of a trial-and-error education for every new owner. A half century or more of the farm's history would be living memory, and its present state of health could be measured against its own past – something exceedingly difficult *outside* of living memory.

A second possibility is that the land would not be overworked to pay for itself at full value with every new owner.

A third possibility would be that, having some confidence in family continuity in place, present owners would have future owners not only in supposition but *in sight* and so would take good care of the land, not for the sake of something so abstract as "the future" or "posterity," but out of particular love for living children and grandchildren.

A fourth possibility is that having the past so immediately in memory, and the future so tangibly in prospect, the human establishment on the land would grow more permanent by the practice of better carpentry and masonry. People who remembered long and well would see the folly of rebuilding their barns every generation or two, and of building new fences every twenty years.

A fifth possibility would be the development of the concept of *enough*. Only long memory can answer, for a given farm or locality, How much land is enough? How much work is enough? How much livestock and crop production is enough? How much power is enough?

A sixth possibility is that of local culture. Who could say what that would be? As members of a society based on the exploitation of its own temporariness, we probably should not venture a guess. But we can perhaps speak with a little competence of how it would begin. It would not be imported from critically approved cultures elsewhere. It would not come from watching certified classics on television. It would begin in work and love. People at work in communities three generations old would know that their bodies renewed, time and again, the movements of other bodies, living and dead, known and loved, remembered and loved, in the same shops, houses, and fields. That, of course, is a description of a kind of community dance. And such a dance is perhaps the best way we have to describe harmony.

MICHELLE CLIFF

A Journey into Speech

The first piece of writing I produced, beyond a dissertation on intellectual game-playing in the Italian Renaissance, was entitled "Notes on Speechlessness," published in *Sinister Wisdom,* no. 5. In it I talked about my identification with Victor, the wild boy of Aveyron, who, after his rescue from the forest and wildness by a well-meaning doctor of Enlightenment Europe, became "civilized," but never came to speech. I felt, with Victor, that my wildness had been tamed – that which I had been taught was my wildness.

My dissertation was produced at the Warburg Institute, University of London, and was responsible for giving me an intellectual belief in myself that I had not had before, while at the same time distancing me from who I am, almost rendering me speechless about who I am. At least I believed in the young woman who wrote the dissertation – still, I wondered who she was and where she had come from.

I could speak fluently, but I could not reveal. I immersed myself in the social circles and academies of Siena, Florence, Urbino, as well as Venice, creating a place for myself there, and describing this ideal world in eloquent linear prose.

When I began, finally, partly through participation in the feminist movement, to approach myself as a subject, my writing was jagged, nonlinear, almost shorthand. The "Notes on

Speechlessness" were indeed notes, written in snatches on a
nine-to-five job. I did not choose the note form consciously; a
combination of things drew me to it. An urgency for one
thing. I also felt incompetent to construct an essay in which I
would describe the intimacies, fears, and lies I wrote of in
"Speechlessness." I felt my thoughts, things I had held within
for a lifetime, traversed so wide a terrain, had so many stops
and starts, apparent non sequiturs, that an essay – with its
cold-blooded dependence on logical construction, which I
had mastered practically against my will – could not work. My
subject could not respond to that form, which would have
contradicted the idea of speechlessness. This tender approach
to myself within the confines and interruptions of a forty-
hour-a-week job and against a history of forced fluency was
the beginning of a journey into speech.

To describe this journey further, I must begin at the very
beginning, with origins, and the significance of these origins.
How they have made me the writer I am.

I originate in the Caribbean, specifically on the island of
Jamaica, and although I have lived in the United States and in
England, I travel as a Jamaican. It is Jamaica that forms my
writing for the most part, and which has formed for the most
part, myself. Even though I often feel what Derek Walcott
expresses in his poem "The Schooner *Flight*": "I had no
nation now but the imagination." It is a complicated business.

Jamaica is a place halfway between Africa and England, to
put it simply, although historically one culture (guess which
one) has been esteemed and the other denigrated (both are
understatements) – at least among those who control the culture and politics of the island – the Afro-Saxons. As a child
among these people, indeed of these people, as one of them, I
received the message of anglocentrism, of white supremacy,
and I internalized it. As a writer, as a human being, I have
had to accept that reality and deal with its effect on me, as well
as finding what has been lost to me from the darker side, and
what may be hidden, to be dredged from memory and dream.
And it *is* there to be dredged. As my writing delved longer

and deeper into this part of myself, I began to dream and imagine. I was able to clearly envision Nanny, the leader of a group of guerrilla fighters known as the Windward Maroons, as she is described: an old Black woman naked except for a necklace made from the teeth of white men. I began to love her.

It is a long way from the court of Urbino to Nanny the Coromantyn warrior. (Coromantyn, or Coromantee, was used by the British in Jamaica to describe slaves from the Gold Coast of Africa, especially slaves who spoke Akan.)

One of the effects of assimilation, indoctrination, passing into the anglocentrism of British West Indian culture is that you believe absolutely in the hegemony of the King's English and in the form in which it is meant to be expressed. Or else your writing is not literature; it is folklore, and folklore can never be art. Read some poetry by West Indian writers – some, not all – and you will see what I mean. You have to dissect stanza after extraordinarily anglican stanza for Afro-Caribbean truth; you may never find the latter. But this has been our education. The anglican ideal – Milton, Wordsworth, Keats – was held before us with an assurance that we were unable, and would never be enabled, to compose a work of similar correctness. No reggae spoken here.

To write as a complete Caribbean woman, or man for that matter, demands of us retracing the African part of ourselves, reclaiming as our own, and as our subject, a history sunk under the sea, or scattered as potash in the canefields, or gone to bush, or trapped in a class system notable for its rigidity and absolute dependence on color stratification. On a past bleached from our minds. It means finding the art forms of these of our ancestors and speaking in the *patois* forbidden us. It means realizing our knowledge will always be wanting. It means also, I think, mixing in the forms taught us by the oppressor, undermining his language and co-opting his style, and turning it to our purpose. In my current work-in-progress, a novel, I alternate the King's English with *patois*, not only to show the class background of characters, but to show

how Jamaicans operate within a split consciousness. It would
be as dishonest to write the novel entirely in *patois* as to write
entirely in the King's English. Neither is the novel a linear
construction; its subject is the political upheavals of the past
twenty years. Therefore, I have mixed time and incident and
space and character and also form to try to mirror the historical turbulence.

For another example, I wrote a long poem, actually half-
poem, half-prose, in which I imagine the visit of Botha of
South Africa to the heads of western Europe in the summer
of 1984. I wrote this as a parody of Gilbert and Sullivan
because their work epitomizes salient aspects of the British
Empire which remain vibrant. And because as a child I was
sick to death of hearing "I am the very model of a modern
major general." I enjoyed writing this, playing with rhyme
and language – it was like spitting into their cultural soup.

We are a fragmented people. My experience as a writer
coming from a culture of colonialism, a culture of Black people riven from each other, my struggle to get wholeness from
fragmentation while working within fragmentation, produc-
ing work which may find its strength in its depiction of fragmentation, through form as well as content, is similar to the
experience of other writers whose origins are in countries
defined by colonialism.

Ama Ata Aidoo, the Ghanaian writer, in her extraordinary
book, *Our Sister Killjoy or Reflections from a Black-Eyed Squint*
(NOK Publishers, Lagos and New York, 1979), plots this
fragmentation, and shows how both the demand and solace
of the so-called mother country can claim us, while we long
for our homeland and are shamed for it and ourselves at the
same time. The form Aidoo uses to depict this dilemma of
colonial peoples – part prose, fictional and epistolary, part
poetry – illustrates the fragmentation of the heroine and
grasps the fury of the heroine, living in Europe but drawn
back to Ghana, knowing she can never be European. She will
only be a been-to; that is, one who has been to the mother
country. *Our Sister Killjoy* affected me directly, not just because

like Aidoo's heroine I was a been-to. I was especially drawn by the way in which Aidoo expresses rage against colonialism – crystallized for her by the white man she calls the "Christian Doctor" throughout, excising Black African hearts to salvage white South African lives. In her expression of the rage she feels her prose breaks apart sharply into a staccato poetry – direct, short, brilliantly bitter – as if measured prose would disintegrate under her fury.

I wanted that kind of directness in my writing, as I came into closer contact with my rage, and a realization that rage could fuel and shape my work. As a light-skinned colonial girlchild, both in Jamaica and in the Jamaican milieu of my family abroad, rage was the last thing expected of me.

After reading Aidoo I knew I wanted to tell exactly how things were, what had been done, to us and by us, without muddying the issue with conventional beauty, avoiding becoming trapped in the grace of language for its own sake, which is always seductive.

In *Claiming an Identity They Taught Me to Despise,* a piece published before I read Aidoo, halfway between poetry and prose, as I am halfway between Africa and England, patriot and expatriate, white and Black, I felt my use of language and imagery had sometimes masked what I wanted to convey. It seemed sometimes that the reader was able to ignore what I was saying while admiring the way in which it was said.

And yet, *Claiming* is an honest self-portrait of who I was at the time. Someone who was unable, for the most part, to recapture the native language of Jamaica, and who relied on the King's English and European allusions, but who wrote from a feminist consciousness and a rapidly evolving consciousness of colonialism, and a knowledge of self-hatred. Someone who also dreamed in Latin – as I did and as I recorded in the title section, included here. *Claiming*'s strengths, I think, are in the more intimate, private places of the piece, which I constructed much as the "Notes on Speechlessness" are constructed. Shorthand – almost – as memory and dream emerge; fast, at once keen, at once incomplete. I was also, in

those sections, laboring under the ancient taboos of the assim-
ilated: don't tell outsiders anything real about yourself. Don't
reveal *our* secrets to *them*. Don't make us seem foolish, or
oppressed. Write it quickly before someone catches you. Before you catch yourself.

After reading *Our Sister Killjoy,* something was set loose in
me, I directed rage outward rather than inward, and I was
able to write a piece called "If I Could Write This in Fire I
Would Write This in Fire." In it I let myself go, any thought
of approval for my words vanished; I strung together myth,
dream, historical detail, observation, as I had done before,
but I added native language, tore into the indoctrination of
the colonizer, surprised myself with the violence of my words.

That piece of writing led to other pieces in which I try to
depict personal fragmentation and describe political reality,
according to the peculiar lens of the colonized.

If I Could Write This in Fire, I Would Write This in Fire

I

We were standing under the waterfall at the top of Orange River. Our chests were just beginning to mound – slight hills on either side. In the center of each were our nipples, which were losing their sideways look and rounding into perceptible buttons of dark flesh. Too fast it seemed. We touched each other, then, quickly and almost simultaneously, raised our arms to examine the hairs growing underneath. Another sign. Mine was wispy and light-brown. My friend Zoe had dark hair curled up tight. In each little patch the riverwater caught the sun so we glistened.

The waterfall had come about when my uncles dammed up the river to bring power to the sugar mill. Usually, when I say "sugar mill" to anyone not familiar with the Jamaican country-side or for that matter my family, I can tell their minds cast an image of tall smokestacks, enormous copper cauldrons, a man in a broad-brimmed hat with a whip, and several dozens of slaves – that is, if they have any idea of how large sugar mills once operated. It's a grandiose expression – like plantation, verandah, out-building. (Try substituting farm, porch, out-side toilet.) To some people it even sounds romantic.

Our sugar mill was little more than a round-roofed shed, which contained a wheel and woodfire. We paid an old man to run it, tend the fire, and then either bartered or gave the sugar away, after my grandmother had taken what she needed. Our canefield was about two acres of flat land next to the river. My grandmother had six acres in all – one donkey, a mule, two cows, some chickens, a few pigs, and stray dogs and cats who had taken up residence in the yard.

Her house had four rooms, no electricity, no running water. The kitchen was a shed in the back with a small pot-bellied stove. Across from the stove was a mahogany counter, which had a white enamel basin set into it. The only light source was a window, a small space covered partly by a wooden shutter. We washed our faces and hands in enamel bowls with cold water carried in kerosene tins from the river and poured from enamel pitchers. Our chamber pots were enamel also, and in the morning we carefully placed them on the steps at the side of the house where my grandmother collected them and disposed of their contents. The outhouse was about thirty yards from the back door – a "closet" as we called it – infested with lizards capable of changing color. When the door was shut it was totally dark, and the lizards made their presence known by the noise of their scurrying through the torn news-paper, or the soft shudder when they dropped from the walls. I remember most clearly the stench of the toilet, which seemed to hang in the air in that climate.

But because every little piece of reality exists in relation to another little piece, our situation was not that simple. It was to our yard that people came with news first. It was in my grand-mother's parlor that the Disciples of Christ held their meetings.

Zoe lived with her mother and sister on borrowed ground in a place called Breezy Hill. She and I saw each other almost every day on our school vacations over a period of three years. Each morning early – as I sat on the cement porch with my coffee cut with condensed milk – she appeared: in her straw hat, school tunic faded from blue to gray, white blouse, sneakers hanging around her neck. We had coffee together, and a piece of hard-dough bread with butter and cheese, waited a bit and headed for the river. At first we were shy with each other. We did not start from the same place.

There was land. My grandparents' farm. And there was color.

(My family was called *red*. A term which signified a degree of whiteness. "We's just a flock of red people," a cousin of mine said once.) In the hierarchy of shades I was considered among the lightest. The countrywomen who visited my grandmother commented on my "tall" hair – meaning long. Wavy, not curly.

I had spent the years from three to ten in New York and spoke – at first – like an American. I wore American clothes: shorts, slacks, bathing suit. Because of my American past I was looked upon as the creator of games. Cowboys and Indians. Cops and Robbers. Peter Pan.

(While the primary colonial identification for Jamaicans was English, American colonialism was a strong force in my childhood – and of course continues today. We were sent American movies and American music. American aluminum companies had already discovered bauxite on the island and were shipping the ore to their mainland. United Fruit bought our bananas. White Americans came to Montego Bay, Ocho Rios, and Kingston for their vacations and their cruise ships docked in Port Antonio and other places. In some ways America was seen as a better place than England by many Jamaicans. The farm laborers sent to work in American agribusiness came home with dollars and gifts and new clothes; there were few who mentioned American racism. Many of the middle class who emigrated to Brooklyn or Staten Island or Manhattan were able to pass into the white American world – saving their blackness for other Jamaicans or for trips home; in some cases, forgetting it altogether. Those middle-class Jamaicans who could not pass for white managed differently – not unlike the Bajans in Paule Marshall's *Brown Girl, Brownstones* – saving, working, investing, buying property. Completely separate in most cases from Black Americans.)

I was someone who had experience with the place that sent us triple features of B-grade westerns and gangster movies. And I had tall hair and light skin. And I was the granddaughter of my grandmother. So I had power. I was the cowboy, Zoe was my sidekick, the boys we knew were Indians. I was the detective, Zoe was my "girl," the boys were the robbers. I was Peter Pan, Zoe was Wendy Darling, the boys were the lost boys. And the terrain around the river – jungled and dark green – was Tombstone, or Chicago, or Never-Never Land.

This place and my friendship with Zoe never touched my life in Kingston. We did not correspond with each other when I left my grandmother's home.

I never visited Zoe's home the entire time I knew her. It was a given: never suggested, never raised.

Zoe went to a state school held in a country church in Red Hills. It had been my mother's school. I went to a private all-girls school where I was taught by white Englishwomen and pale Jamaicans. In her school the students were caned as punishment. In mine the harshest punishment I remember was being sent to sit under the *lignum vitae* to "commune with nature." Some of the girls were out-and-out white (English and American), the rest of us were colored – only a few were dark. Our uniforms were blood-red gabardine, heavy and hot. Classes were held in buildings meant to recreate England: damp with stone floors, facing onto a cloister, or quad as they called it. We began each day with the headmistress leading us in English hymns. The entire school stood for an hour in the zinc-roofed gymnasium.

Occasionally a girl fainted, or threw up. Once, a girl had a grand mal seizure. To any such disturbance the response was always "keep singing." While she flailed on the stone floor, I wondered what the mistresses would do. We sang "Faith of Our Fathers," and watched our classmate as her eyes rolled back in her head. I thought of people swallowing their tongues. This student was dark – here on a scholarship – and the only woman who came forward to help her was the gamesmistress, the only dark teacher. She kneeled beside the girl and slid the white web belt from her tennis shorts, clamping it between the girl's teeth. When the seizure was over, she carried the girl to a tumbling mat in a corner of the gym and covered her so she wouldn't get chilled.

Were the other women unable to touch this girl because of her darkness? I think that now. Her darkness and her scholarship. She lived on Windward Road with her grandmother; her mother was a maid. But darkness is usually enough for women like those to hold back. Then, we usually excused that kind of behavior by saying they were "ladies." (We were constantly being told we should be ladies also. One teacher went so far as to tell us many people thought Jamaicans lived in trees and we had to show these people they were mistaken.) In short, we felt insufficient to judge the behavior of these women. The English ones (who had the corner on power in the school) had come all this way to teach us. Shouldn't we treat them as the missionaries they were certain they were? The creole Jamaicans had a different role: they were passing on to those of us who were light-skinned the creole heritage of collaboration, assimilation, loyalty to our betters. We were expected to be willing subjects in this outpost of civilization.

The girl left school that day and never returned.

After prayers we filed into our classrooms. After classes we had games: tennis, field hockey, rounders (what the English call baseball), netball (what the English call basketball). For games we were divided into "houses" – groups named for Joan of Arc, Edith Cavell, Florence Nightingale, Jane Austen. Four white heroines. Two martyrs. One saint. Two nurses. (None of us knew then that there were Black women with Nightingale at Scutari.) One novelist. Three involved in white men's wars. Two dead in white men's wars. *Pride and Prejudice.*

Those of us in Cavell wore red badges and recited her last words before a firing squad in W. W. I: "Patriotism is not enough. I must have no hatred or bitterness toward anyone."

Sorry to say I grew up to have exactly that.

Looking back: To try and see when the background changed places with the foreground. To try and locate the vanishing point: where the lines of perspective converge and disappear. Lines of color and class. Lines of history and social context. Lines of denial and rejection. When did *we* (the light-skinned middle-class Jamaicans) take over for *them* as oppressors? I need to see when and how this happened. When what should have been reality was overtaken by what was surely unreality. When the house nigger became master.

"What's the matter with you? You think you're white or some-thing?"
"Child, what you want to know 'bout Garvey for? The man was nothing but a damn fool."
"They not our kind of people."
Why did we wear wide-brimmed hats and try to get into Oxford? Why did we not return?

Great Expectations: a novel about origins and denial. about the futility and tragedy of that denial. about attempting assimila-tion. We learned this novel from a light-skinned Jamaican woman – she concentrated on what she called the "love affair" between Pip and Estella.

Looking back: Through the last page of *Sula.* "And the loss pressed down on her chest and came up into her throat. 'We was girls together,' she said as though explaining something." It was Zoe, and Zoe alone, I thought of. She snapped into my mind and I remembered no one else. Through the greens and blues of the riverbank. The flame of red hibiscus in front of my grandmother's house. The cracked grave of a former landowner. The fruit of the ackee which poisons those who don't know how to prepare it.

"What is to become of us?"
We borrowed a baby from a woman and used her as our dolly. Dressed and undressed her. Dipped her in the riverwater. Fed her with the milk her mother had left with us: and giggled because we knew where the milk had come from.

A letter: "I am desperate. I need to get away. I beg you one fifty-dollar."

I send the money because this is what she asks for. I visit her on a trip back home. Her front teeth are gone. Her husband beats her and she suffers blackouts. I sit on her chair. She is given birth control pills which aggravate her "condition." We boil up sorrel and ginger. She is being taught by Peace Corps volunteers to embroider linen mats with little lambs on them and gives me one as a keepsake. We cool off the sorrel with a block of ice brought from the shop nearby. The shopkeeper immediately recognizes me as my grandmother's granddaughter and refuses to sell me cigarettes. (I am twentyseven.) We sit in the doorway of her house, pushing back the colored plastic strands which form a curtain, and talk about Babylon and Dred. About Manley and what he's doing for Jamaica. About how hard it is. We walk along the railway tracks – no longer used – to Crooked River and the post

office. Her little daughter walks beside us and we recite a
poem for her: "Mornin' buddy/Me no buddy fe wunna/Who
den, den I saw?" and on and on.

I can come and go. And I leave. To complete my education in
London.

II

Their goddam kings and their goddam queens. Grandmoth-
erly Victoria spreading herself thin across the globe. Elizabeth II on our TV screens. We stop what we are doing. We
quiet down. We pay our respects.

1981: In Massachusetts I get up at 5 a.m. to watch the royal
wedding. I tell myself maybe the IRA will intervene. It's got to
be better than starving themselves to death. Better to be a
kamikaze in St. Paul's Cathedral than a hostage in Ulster. And
last week Black and white people smashed storefronts all over
the United Kingdom. But I really don't believe we'll see royal
blood on TV. I watch because they once ruled us. In the back
of the cathedral a Maori woman sings an aria from Handel,
and I notice that she is surrounded by the colored subjects.

To those of us in the commonwealth the royal family was the
perfect symbol of hegemony. To those of us who were dark in
the dark nations, the prime minister, the parliament barely
existed. We believed in royalty – we were convinced in this
belief. Maybe it played on some ancestral memories of West
Africa – where other kings and queens had been. Altars and
castles and magic.

The faces of our new rulers were everywhere in my childhood. Calendars, newsreels, magazines. Their presences were
often among us. Attending test matches between the West
Indians and South Africans. They were our landlords. Not
always absentee. And no matter what Black leader we might

elect – were we to choose independence – we would be losing something almost holy in our impudence.

WE ARE HERE BECAUSE YOU WERE THERE
BLACK PEOPLE AGAINST STATE BRUTALITY
BLACK WOMEN WILL NOT BE INTIMIDATED
WELCOME TO BRITAIN . . . WELCOME TO SECOND-
CLASS CITIZENSHIP
(slogans of the Black movement in Britain)

Indian women cleaning the toilets in Heathrow airport. This is the first thing I notice. Dark women in saris trudging buckets back and forth as other dark women in saris – some covered by loosefitting winter coats – form a line to have their passports stamped.

The triangle trade: molasses/rum/slaves. Robinson Crusoe was on a slave-trading journey. Robert Browning was a mulatto. Holding pens. Jamaica was a seasoning station. Split tongues. Sliced ears. Whipped bodies. The constant pretense of civility against rape. Still. Iron collars. Tinplate masks. The latter a precaution: to stop the slaves from eating the sugar cane.

A pregnant woman is to be whipped – they dig a hole to accommodate her belly and place her face down on the ground. Many of us became light-skinned very fast. Traced ourselves through bastard lines to reach the duke of Devonshire. The earl of Cornwall. The lord of this and the lord of that. Our mothers' rapes were the things unspoken.

You say: But Britain freed her slaves in 1833. Yes.

Tea plantations in India and Ceylon. Mines in Africa. The Cape-to-Cairo Railroad. Rhodes scholars. Suez Crisis. The white man's bloody burden. Boer War. Bantustans. Sitting in a theatre in London in the seventies. A play called *West of Suez*. A lousy play about British colonials. The finale comes when several well-known white actors are machine-gunned by several lesser-known Black actors. (As Nina Simone says: "This is a show tune but the show hasn't been written for it yet.")

The red empire of geography classes. "The sun never sets on the British empire and you can't trust it in the dark." Or with the dark peoples. "Because of the Industrial Revolution European countries went in search of markets and raw materials." Another geography (or was it a history) lesson.

Their bloody kings and their bloody queens. Their bloody peers. Their bloody generals. Admirals. Explorers. Livingstone. Hillary. Kitchener. All the bwanas. And all their beaters, porters, sherpas. Who found the source of the Nile. Victoria Falls. The tops of mountains. Their so-called discoveries reek of untruth. How many dark people died so they could misname the physical features in their blasted gazetteer. A statistic we shall never know. Dr. Livingstone, I presume you are here to rape our land and enslave our people.

There are statues of these dead white men all over London.

An interesting fact: The swear word "bloody" is a contraction of "by my lady" – a reference to the Virgin Mary. They do tend to use their ladies. Name ages for them. Places for them. Use them as screens, inspirations, symbols. And many of the ladies comply. While the national martyr Edith Cavell was being executed by the Germans in 1915 in Belgium (called "poor little Belgium" by the allies in the war), the Belgians were engaged in the exploitation of the land and peoples of the Congo.

And will we ever know how many dark peoples were "imported" to fight in white men's wars. Probably not. Just as we will never know how many hearts were cut from African people so that the Christian doctor might be a success – i.e., extend a white man's life. Our Sister Killjoy observes this from her black-eyed squint.

Dr. Schweitzer – humanitarian, authority on Bach, winner of the Nobel Peace Prize – on the people of Africa: "The Negro is a child, and with children nothing can be done without the use of authority. We must, therefore, so arrange the circumstances of our daily life that my authority can find expression. With regard to Negroes, then, I have coined the formula: 'I am your brother, it is true, but your elder brother.' " (*On the Edge of the Primeval Forest*, 1961)

They like to pretend we didn't fight back. We did: with obeah, poison, revolution. It simply was not enough.

"Colonies . . . these places where 'niggers' are cheap and the earth is rich." (W.E.B. DuBois, "The Souls of White Folk")

A cousin is visiting me from Cal Tech where he is getting a degree in engineering. I am learning about the Italian Renaissance. My cousin is recognizably Black and speaks with an accent. I am not and do not – unless I am back home, where the "twang" comes upon me. We sit for some time in a bar in his hotel and are not served. A light-skinned Jamaican comes over to our table. He is an older man – a professor at the University of London. "Don't bother with it, you hear. They don't serve us in this bar." A run-of-the-mill incident for all recognizably Black people in this city. But for me it is not.

Henry's eyes fill up, but he refuses to believe our informant. "No, man, the girl is just busy." (The girl is a fifty-year-old white woman, who may just be following orders. But I do not mention this. I have chosen sides.) All I can manage to say is, "Jesus Christ, I hate the fucking English." Henry looks at me. (In the family I am known as the "lady cousin." It has to do with how I look. And the fact that I am twenty-seven and unmarried – and for all they know, unattached. They do not know that I am really the lesbian cousin.) Our informant says – gently, but with a distinct tone of disappointment – "My dear, is that what you're studying at the university?"

You see – the whole business is very complicated.

Henry and I leave without drinks and go to meet some of his white colleagues at a restaurant I know near Covent Garden Opera House. The restaurant caters to theatre types and so I hope there won't be a repeat of the bar scene – at least they know how to pretend. Besides, I tell myself, the owners are Italian *and* gay; they *must* be halfway decent. Henry and his colleagues work for an American company which is paying their way through Cal Tech. They mine bauxite from the hills in the middle of the island and send it to the United States. A turnaround occurs at dinner: Henry joins the white men in a sustained mockery of the waiters: their accents and the way they walk. He whispers to me: "Why you want to bring us to a battyman's den, lady?" (*Battyman = faggot* in Jamaican.) I keep quiet.

We put the white men in a taxi and Henry walks me to the underground station. He asks me to sleep with him. (It wouldn't be incest. His mother was a maid in the house of an uncle and Henry has not seen her since his birth. He was taken into the family. She was let go.) I say that I can't. I plead exams. I can't say that I don't want to. Because I remember what happened in the bar. But I can't say that I'm a lesbian either – even though I want to believe his alliance with the white men at dinner was forced: not really him. He doesn't buy my excuse. "Come on, lady, let's do it. What's the matter, you 'fraid?" I pretend I am back home and start patois to show him somehow I am not afraid, not English, not white. I tell him he's a married man and he tells me he's a ram goat. I take the train to where I am staying and try to forget the whole thing. But I don't. I remember our different skins and our different experiences within them. And I have a hard time realizing that I am angry with Henry. That to him – no use in pretending – a queer is a queer.

1981: I hear on the radio that Bob Marley is dead and I drive over the Mohawk Trail listening to a program of his music and I cry and cry and cry. Someone says: "It wasn't the ganja that killed him, it was poverty and working in a steel foundry when he was young."

I flash back to my childhood and a young man who worked for an aunt I lived with once. He taught me to smoke ganja behind the house. And to peel an orange with the tip of a machete without cutting through the skin – "Love" it was called: a necklace of orange rind the result. I think about him because I heard he had become a Rastaman. And then I think about Rastas.

We are sitting on the porch of an uncle's house in Kingston – the family and I – and a Rastaman comes to the gate. We have guns but they are locked behind a false closet. We have dogs but they are tied up. We are Jamaicans and know that Rastas mean no harm. We let him in and he sits on the side of the porch and shows us his brooms and brushes. We buy some to take back to New York. "Peace, missis."

There were many Rastas in my childhood. Walking the roadside with their goods. Sitting outside their shacks in the mountains. The outsides painted bright – sometimes with words. Gathering at Palisadoes Airport to greet the Conquering Lion of Judah. They were considered figures of fun by most middle-class Jamaicans. Harmless – like Marcus Garvey.

Later: white American hippies trying to create the effect of dred in their straight white hair. The ganja joint held between their straight white teeth. "Man, the grass is good." Hanging

out by the Sheraton pool. Light-skinned Jamaicans also dred-
locked, also assuming the ganja. Both groups moving to the
music but not the words. Harmless. "Peace, brother."

III

My grandmother: "Let us thank God for a fruitful place."
My grandfather: "Let us rescue the perishing world."

This evening on the road in western Massachusetts there are
pockets of fog. Then clear spaces. Across from a pond a dog
staggers in front of my headlights. I look closer and see that
his mouth is foaming. He stumbles to the side of the road – I
go to call the police.

I drive back to the house, radio playing "difficult" piano
pieces. And I think about how I need to say all this. This is
who I am. I am not what you allow me to be. Whatever you
decide me to be. In a bookstore in London I show the woman
at the counter my book and she stares at me for a minute,
then says: "You're a Jamaican." "Yes." "You're not at all like
our Jamaicans."

Encountering the void is nothing more nor less than understanding invisibility. Of being fogbound.

Then: It was never a question of passing. It was a question
         of hiding. Behind Black and white perceptions of
         who we were – who they thought we were. Tropics.
         Plantations. Calypso. Cricket. We were the people
         with the musical voices and the coronation mugs on
         our parlor tables. I would be whatever figure these
         foreign imaginations cared for me to be. It would be
         so simple to let others fill in for me. So easy to startle
         them with a flash of anger when their visions got out
         of hand – but never to sustain the anger for myself.

It could become a life lived within myself. A life cut off. I know who I am but you will never know who I am. I may in fact lose touch with who I am.

I hid from my real sources. But my real sources were also hidden from me.

Now: It is not a question of relinquishing privilege. It is a question of grasping more of myself. I have found that in the real sources are concealed my survival. My speech. My voice. To be colonized is to be rendered insensitive. To have those parts necessary to sustain life numbed. And this is in some cases – in my case – perceived as privilege. The test of a colonized person is to walk through a shantytown in Kingston and not bat an eye. This I cannot do. Because part of me lives there – and as I grasp more of this part I realize what needs to be done with the rest of my life.

Sometimes I used to think we were like the Marranos – the Sephardic Jews forced to pretend they were Christians. The name was given to them by the Christians, and meant "pigs." But once out of Spain and Portugal, they became Jews openly again. Some settled in Jamaica. They knew who the enemy was and acted for their own survival. But they remained Jews always.

We also knew who the enemy was – I remember jokes about the English. Saying they stank. saying they were stingy. that they drank too much and couldn't hold their liquor. that they had bad teeth. were dirty and dishonest. were limey bastards. and horse-faced bitches. We said the men only wanted to sleep with Jamaican women. And that the women made pigs of themselves with Jamaican men.

But of course this was seen by us – the light-skinned middle class – with a double vision. We learned to cherish that part of us that was them – and to deny the part that was not. Believing in some cases that the latter part had ceased to exist.

None of this is as simple as it may sound. We were colorists and we aspired to oppressor status. (Of course, almost any aspiration instilled by Western civilization is to oppressor status: success, for example.) Color was the symbol of our potential: color taking in hair "quality," skin tone, freckles, nose-width, eyes. We did not see that color symbolism was a method of keeping us apart: in the society, in the family, between friends. Those of us who were light-skinned, straight-haired, etc., were given to believe that we could actually attain whiteness – or at least those qualities of the colonizer which made him superior. We were convinced of white supremacy. If we failed, we were not really responsible for our failures: we had all the advantages – but it was that one persistent drop of blood, that single rogue gene that made us unable to conceptualize abstract ideas, made us love darkness rather than despise it, which was to be blamed for our failure. Our dark part had taken over: an inherited imbalance in which the doom of the creole was sealed.

I am trying to write this as clearly as possible, but as I write I realize that what I say may sound fabulous, or even mythic. It is. It is insane.

Under this system of colorism – the system which prevailed in my childhood in Jamaica, and which has carried over to the present – rarely will dark and light people co-mingle. Rarely will they achieve between themselves an intimacy informed with identity. (I should say here that I am using the categories light and dark both literally and symbolically. There are dark Jamaicans who have achieved lightness and the "advantages" which go with it by their successful pursuit of oppressor status.)

Under this sytem light and dark people will meet in those ways in which the light-skinned person imitates the oppressor. But imitation goes only so far: the light-skinned person becomes an oppressor in fact. He/she will have a dark chauffeur, a dark nanny, a dark maid, and a dark gardener. These employees will be paid badly. Because of the slave past, because of their dark skin, the servants of the middle class have been used according to the traditions of the slavocracy. They are not seen as workers for their own sake, but for the sake of the family who has employed them. It was not until Michael Manley became prime minister that a minimum wage for houseworkers was enacted – and the indignation of the middle class was profound.

During Manley's leadership the middle class began to abandon the island in droves. Toronto. Miami. New York. Leaving their houses and businesses behind and sewing cash into the tops of suitcases. Today – with a new regime – they are returning: "Come back to the way things used to be" the tourist advertisement on American TV says. "Make it Jamaica again. Make it your own."

But let me return to the situation of houseservants as I remember it: They will be paid badly, but they will be "given" room and board. However, the key to the larder will be kept by the mistress in her dresser drawer. They will spend Christmas with the family of their employers and be given a length of English wool for trousers or a few yards of cotton for dresses. They will see their children on their days off: their extended family will care for the children the rest of the time. When the employers visit their relations in the country, the servants may be asked along – oftentimes the servants of the middle class come from the same part of the countryside their employers have come from. But they will be expected to work while they are there. Back in town, there are parts of the house they are allowed to move freely around; other parts they are not allowed to enter. When the family watches the

TV the servant is allowed to watch also, but only while standing in a doorway. The servant may have a radio in his/her room, also a dresser and a cot. Perhaps a mirror. There will usually be one ceiling light. And one small square louvered window.

A true story: One middle-class Jamaican woman ordered a Persian rug from Harrod's in London. The day it arrived so did her new maid. She was going downtown to have her hair touched up, and told the maid to vacuum the rug. She told the maid she would find the vacuum cleaner in the same shed as the power mower. And when she returned she found that the fine nap of her new rug had been removed.

The reaction of the mistress was to tell her friends that the "girl" was backward. She did not fire her until she found that the maid had scrubbed the teflon from her new set of pots, saying she thought they were coated with "nastiness."

The houseworker/mistress relationship in which one Black woman is the oppressor of another Black woman is a cornerstone of the experience of many Jamaican women.

I remember another true story: In a middle-class family's home one Christmas, a relation was visiting from New York. This woman had brought gifts for everybody, including the housemaid. The maid had been released from a mental institution recently, where they had "treated" her for depression. This visiting light-skinned woman had brought the dark woman a bright red rayon blouse and presented it to her in the garden one afternoon, while the family was having tea. The maid thanked her softly, and the other woman moved toward her as if to embrace her. Then she stopped, her face suddenly covered with tears, and ran into the house, saying, "My God, I can't, I can't."

We are women who come from a place almost incredible in its beauty. It is a beauty which can mask a great deal and which has been used in that way. But that the beauty is there is a fact. I remember what I thought the freedom of my childhood, in which the fruitful place was something I took for granted. Just as I took for granted Zoe's appearance every morning on my school vacations – in the sense that I knew she would be there. That she would always be the one to visit me. The perishing world of my grandfather's graces at the table, if I ever seriously thought about it, was somewhere else.

Our souls were affected by the beauty of Jamaica, as much as they were affected by our fears of darkness.

There is no ending to this piece of writing. There is no way to end it. As I read back over it, I see that we/they/I may become confused in the mind of the reader: but these pronouns have always co-existed in my mind. The Rastas talk of the "I and I" – a pronoun in which they combine themselves with Jah. Jah is a contraction of Jahweh and Jehova, but to me always sounds like the beginning of Jamaica. I and Jamaica is who I am. No matter how far I travel – how deep the ambivalence I feel about ever returning. And Jamaica is a place in which we/they/I connect and disconnect – change place.

CARLOS FUENTES

How I Started to Write

I

I was born on November 11, 1928, under the sign I would have chosen, Scorpio, and on a date shared with Dostoevsky, Crommelynck, and Vonnegut. My mother was rushed from a steaming-hot movie house in those days before Colonel Buendía took his son to discover ice in the tropics. She was seeing King Vidor's version of *La Bohème* with John Gilbert and Lillian Gish. Perhaps the pangs of my birth were provoked by this anomaly: a silent screen version of Puccini's opera. Since then, the operatic and the cinematographic have had a tug-of-war with my words, as if expecting the Scorpio of fiction to rise from silent music and blind images.

All this, let me add to clear up my biography, took place in the sweltering heat of Panama City, where my father was beginning his diplomatic career as an attaché to the Mexican legation. (In those days, embassies were established only in the most important capitals – no place where the mean average year-round temperature was perpetually in the nineties.) Since my father was a convinced Mexican nationalist, the problem of where I was to be born had to be resolved under the sign, not of Scorpio, but of the Eagle and the Serpent.

The Mexican legation, however, though it had extraterritorial rights, did not have even a territorial midwife; and the minister, a fastidious bachelor from Sinaloa by the name of Ignacio Norris, who resembled the poet Quevedo as one pince-nez resembles another, would have none of me suddenly appearing on the legation parquet, even if the Angel Gabriel had announced me as a future Mexican writer of some, albeit debatable, merit.

So if I could not be born in a fictitious, extraterritorial Mexico, neither would I be born in that even more fictitious extension of the United States of America, the Canal Zone, where, naturally, the best hospitals were. So, between two territorial fictions – the Mexican legation, the Canal Zone – and a mercifully silent close-up of John Gilbert, I arrived in the nick of time at the Gorgas Hospital in Panama City at eleven that evening.

The problem of my baptism then arose. As if the waters of the two neighboring oceans touching each other with the iron fingertips of the canal were not enough, I had to undergo a double ceremony: my religious baptism took place in Panama, because my mother, a devout Roman Catholic, demanded it with as much urgency as Tristram Shandy's parents, although through less original means. My national baptism took place a few months later in Mexico City, where my father, an incorrigible Jacobin and priest-eater to the end, insisted that I be registered in the civil rolls established by Benito Juárez. Thus, I appear as a native of Mexico City for all legal purposes, and this anomaly further illustrates a central fact of my life and my writing: I am Mexican by will and by imagination.

All this came to a head in the 1930s. By then, my father was counselor of the Mexican Embassy in Washington, D.C., and I grew up in the vibrant world of the American thirties, more or less between the inauguration of Citizen Roosevelt and the interdiction of Citizen Kane. When I arrived here, Dick Tracy had just met Tess Trueheart. As I left, Clark Kent was meeting Lois Lane. You are what you eat. You are also the comics you peruse as a child.

At home, my father made me read Mexican history, study Mexican geography, and understand the names, the dreams and defeats of Mexico: a nonexistent country, I then thought, invented by my father to nourish my infant imagination with yet another marvelous fiction: a land of Oz with a green cactus road, a landscape and a soul so different from those of the United States that they seemed a fantasy.

A cruel fantasy: the history of Mexico was a history of crushing defeats, whereas I lived in a world, that of my D.C. public school, which celebrated victories, one victory after another, from Yorktown to New Orleans to Chapultepec to Appomattox to San Juan Hill to Belleau Wood: had this nation ever known defeat? Sometimes the names of United States victories were the same as the names of Mexico's defeats and humiliations: Monterrey. Veracruz. Chapultepec. Indeed: from the Halls of Montezuma to the shores of Tripoli. In the map of my imagination, as the United States expanded westward, Mexico contracted southward. Miguel Hidalgo, the father of Mexican independence, ended up with his head on exhibit on a lance at the city gates of Chihuahua. Imagine George and Martha beheaded at Mount Vernon.

To the south, sad songs, sweet nostalgia, impossible desires. To the north, self-confidence, faith in progress, boundless optimism. Mexico, the imaginary country, dreamed of a painful past; the United States, the real country, dreamed of a happy future.

The French equate intelligence with rational discourse, the Russians with intense soul-searching. For a Mexican, intelligence is inseparable from maliciousness – in this, as in many other things, we are quite Italian: *furberia,* roguish slyness, and the cult of appearances, *la bella figura,* are Italianate traits present everywhere in Latin America: Rome, more than Madrid, is our spiritual capital in this sense.

For me, as a child, the United States seemed a world where intelligence was equated with energy, zest, enthusiasm. The North American world blinds us with its energy; we cannot see ourselves, we must see *you.* The United States is a world full of cheerleaders, prize-giving, singin' in the rain: the baton twirler, the Oscar awards, the musical comedies cannot be repeated elsewhere; in Mexico, the Hollywood statuette would come dipped in poisoned paint; in France, Gene Kelly would constantly stop in his steps to reflect: *Je danse, donc je suis.*

Many things impressed themselves on me during those years. The United States – would you believe it? – was a country where things worked, where nothing ever broke down: trains, plumbing, roads, punctuality, personal security seemed to function perfectly, at least on the eye level of a young Mexican diplomat's son living in a residential hotel on Washington's Sixteenth Street, facing Meridian Hill Park, where nobody was then mugged and where our superb furnished seven-room apartment cost us 110 pre-inflation dollars a month. Yes, in spite of all the problems, the livin' seemed easy during those long Tidewater summers when I became perhaps the first and only Mexican to prefer grits to guacamole. I also became the original Mexican Calvinist: an invisible taskmaster called Puritanical Duty shadows my every footstep: I shall not deserve anything unless I work relentlessly for it, with iron discipline, day after day. Sloth is sin, and if I do not sit at my typewriter every day at 8 a.m. for a working day of seven to eight hours, I will surely go to hell. No *siestas* for me, alas and alack and *hélas* and *ay-ay-ay*: how I came to envy my Latin brethren, unburdened by the Protestant work ethic, and why must I, to this very day, read the complete works of Hermann Broch and scribble in my black notebook on a sunny Mexican beach, instead of lolling the day away and waiting for the coconuts to fall?

But the United States in the thirties went far beyond my personal experience. The nation that Tocqueville had destined to share dominance over half the world realized that, in effect, only a continental state could be a modern state; in the thirties, the U.S.A. had to decide *what to do* with its new worldwide power, and Franklin Roosevelt taught us to believe that the first thing was for the United States to show that it was capable of living up to its ideals. I learned then – my first political lesson – that this is your true greatness, not, as was to be the norm in my lifetime, material wealth, not arrogant power misused against weaker peoples, not ignorant ethnocentrism burning itself out in contempt for others.

As a young Mexican growing up in the U.S., I had a primary impression of a nation of boundless energy, imagination, and the will to confront and solve the great social issues of the times without blinking or looking for scapegoats. It was the impression of a country identified with its own highest principles: political democracy, economic well-being, and faith in its human resources, especially in that most precious of all capital, the renewable wealth of education and research.

Franklin Roosevelt, then, restored America's self-respect in this essential way, not by macho posturing. I saw the United States in the thirties lift itself by its bootstraps from the dead dust of Oklahoma and the gray lines of the unemployed in Detroit, and this image of health was reflected in my daily life, in my reading of Mark Twain, in the images of movies and newspapers, in the North American capacity for mixing fluffy illusion and hard-bitten truth, self-celebration and self-criticism: the madcap heiresses played by Carole Lombard coexisted with the Walker Evans photographs of hungry, old-at-thirty migrant mothers, and the nimble tread of the feet of Fred Astaire did not silence the heavy stomp of the boots of Tom Joad.

My school – a public school, nonconfessional and coeducational – reflected these realities and their basically egalitarian thrust. I believed in the democratic simplicity of my teachers and chums, and above all I believed I was, naturally, in a totally unself-conscious way, a part of that world. It is important, at all ages and in all occupations, to be "popular" in the United States; I have known no other society where the values of "regularity" are so highly prized. I was popular, I was "regular." Until a day in March – March 18, 1938. On that day, a man from another world, the imaginary country of my childhood, the president of Mexico, Lázaro Cárdenas, nationalized the holdings of foreign oil companies. The headlines in the North American press denounced the "communist" government of Mexico and its "red" president; they demanded the invasion of Mexico in the sacred name of private property, and Mexicans, under international boycott, were invited to drink their oil.

Instantly, surprisingly, I became a pariah in my school. Cold shoulders, aggressive stares, epithets, and sometimes blows. Children know how to be cruel, and the cruelty of their elders is the surest residue of the malaise the young feel toward things strange, things other, things that reveal our own ignorance or insufficiency. This was not reserved for me or for Mexico: at about the same time, an extremely brilliant boy of eleven arrived from Germany. He was a Jew and his family had fled from the Nazis. I shall always remember his face, dark and trembling, his aquiline nose and deep-set, bright eyes with their great sadness; the sensitivity of his hands and the strangeness of it all to his American companions. This young man, Hans Berliner, had a brilliant mathematical mind and he walked and saluted like a Central European; he wore short pants and high woven stockings, Tyrolean jackets and an air of displaced courtesy that infuriated the popular, regular, feisty, knickered, provincial, Depression-era little sons of bitches at Henry Cooke Public School on Thirteenth Street N.W.

The shock of alienation and the shock of recognition are sometimes one and the same. What was different made others afraid, less of what was different than of themselves, of their own incapacity to recognize themselves in the alien.

I discovered that my father's country was real. And that I belonged to it. Mexico was my identity yet I lacked an identity; Hans Berliner suffered more than I – headlines from Mexico are soon forgotten; another great issue becomes all-important for a wonderful ten days' media feast – yet he had an identity as a Central European Jew. I do not know what became of him. Over the years, I have always expected to see him receive a Nobel Prize in one of the sciences. Surely, if he lived, he integrated himself into North American society. I had to look at the photographs of President Cárdenas: he was a man of another lineage; he did not appear in the repertory of glossy, seductive images of the salable North American world. He was a mestizo, Spanish and Indian, with a faraway, green, and liquid look in his eyes, as if he were trying to remember a mute and ancient past.

Was that past mine as well? Could I dream the dreams of the country suddenly revealed in a political act as something more than a demarcation of frontiers on a map or a hillock of statistics in a yearbook? I believe I then had the intuition that I would not rest until I came to grips myself with that common destiny which depended upon still another community: the community of time. The United States had made me believe that we live only for the future; Mexico, Cárdenas, the events of 1938, made me understand that only in an act of the present can we make present the past as well as the future: to be a Mexican was to identify a hunger for being, a desire for dignity rooted in many forgotten centuries and in many centuries yet to come, but rooted here, now, in the instant, in the vigilant time of Mexico I later learned to understand in the stone serpents of Teotihuacán and in the polychrome angels of Oaxaca.

Of course, as happens in childhood, all these deep musings had no proof of existence outside an act that was, more than a prank, a kind of affirmation. In 1939, my father took me to see a film at the old RKO–Keith in Washington. It was called *Man of Conquest* and it starred Richard Dix as Sam Houston. When Dix/Houston proclaimed the secession of the Republic of Texas from Mexico, I jumped on the theater seat and proclaimed on my own and from the full height of my nationalist ten years, "Viva México! Death to the gringos!" My embarrassed father hauled me out of the theater, but his pride in me could not resist leaking my first rebellious act to the *Washington Star*. So I appeared for the first time in a newspaper and became a child celebrity for the acknowledged ten-day span. I read Andy Warhol *avant l'air-brush*: Everyone shall be famous for at least five minutes.

In the wake of my father's diplomatic career, I traveled to
Chile and entered fully the universe of the Spanish language,
of Latin American politics and its adversities. President Roosevelt had resisted enormous pressures to apply sanctions and
even invade Mexico to punish my country for recovering its
own wealth. Likewise, he did not try to destabilize the Chilean
radicals, communists, and socialists democratically elected to
power in Chile under the banners of the Popular Front. In
the early forties, the vigor of Chile's political life was conta-
gious: active unions, active parties, electoral campaigns all
spoke of the political health of this, the most democratic of
Latin American nations. Chile was a politically verbalized
country. It was no coincidence that it was also the country of
the great Spanish-American poets Gabriela Mistral, Vicente
Huidobro, Pablo Neruda.

I only came to know Neruda and became his friend many
years later. This King Midas of poetry would write, in his literary testament rescued from a gutted house and a nameless
tomb, a beautiful song to the Spanish language. The Conquistadors, he said, took our gold, but they left us their gold: they
left us our words. Neruda's gold, I learned in Chile, was the
property of all. One afternoon on the beach at Lota in southern Chile, I saw the miners as they came out, mole-like, from
their hard work many feet under the sea, extracting the coal
of the Pacific Ocean. They sat around a bonfire and sang, to
guitar music, a poem from Neruda's *Canto General*. I told
them that the author would be thrilled to know that his poem
had been set to music.

What author? they asked me in surprise. For them, Neruda's poetry had no author, it came from afar, it had always
been sung, like Homer's. It was the poetry, as Croce said of
the *Iliad*, "d'un popolo intero poetante," of an entire poetiz-
ing people. It was the document of the original identity of
poetry and history.

I learned in Chile that Spanish could be the language of
free men. I was also to learn in my lifetime, in Chile in 1973,
the fragility of both our language and our freedom when

Richard Nixon, unable to destroy American democracy, merrily helped to destroy Chilean democracy, the same thing Leonid Brezhnev had done in Czechoslovakia.

An anonymous language, a language that belongs to us all, as Neruda's poem belonged to those miners on the beach, yet a language that can be kidnapped, impoverished, sometimes jailed, sometimes murdered. Let me summarize this paradox: Chile offered me and the other writers of my generation in Santiago both the essential fragility of a cornered language, Spanish, and the protection of the Latin of our times, the lingua franca of the modern world, the English language. At the Grange School, under the awesome beauty of the Andes, José Donoso and Jorge Edwards, Roberto Torretti, the late Luis Alberto Heyremans, and myself, by then all budding amateurs, wrote our first exercises in literature within this mini-Britannia. We all ran strenuous cross-country races, got caned from time to time, and recuperated while reading Swinburne; and we were subjected to huge doses of rugby, Ruskin, porridge for breakfast, and a stiff upper lip in military defeats. But when Montgomery broke through at El Alamein, the assembled school tossed caps in the air and hip-hip-hoorayed to death. In South America, clubs were named after George Canning and football teams after Lord Cochrane; no matter that English help in winning independence led to English economic imperialism, from oil in Mexico to railways in Argentina. There was a secret thrill in our hearts: our Spanish conquerors had been beaten by the English; the defeat of Philip II's invincible Armada compensated for the crimes of Cortés, Pizarro, and Valdivia. If Britain was an empire, at least she was a democratic one.

In Washington, I had begun writing a personal magazine in English, with my own drawings, book reviews, and epochal bits of news. It consisted of a single copy, penciled and crayonned, and its circulation was limited to our apartment building. Then, at age fourteen, in Chile, I embarked on a more ambitious project, along with my schoolmate Roberto Torretti: a vast Caribbean saga that was to culminate in Haiti on a hilltop palace (Sans Souci?) where a black tyrant kept a mad French mistress in a garret. All this was set in the early nineteenth century and in the final scene (Shades of Jane Eyre! Reflections on Rebecca! Fans of Joan Fontaine!) the palace was to burn down, along with the world of slavery.

But where to begin? Torretti and I were, along with our literary fraternity at The Grange, avid readers of Dumas *père*. A self-respecting novel, in our view, had to start in Marseilles, in full view of the Chateau d'If and the martyrdom of Edmond Dantès. But we were writing in Spanish, not in French, and our characters had to speak Spanish. But, what Spanish? My Mexican Spanish, or Roberto's Chilean Spanish? We came to a sort of compromise: the characters would speak like Andalusians. This was probably a tacit homage to the land from which Columbus sailed.

The Mexican painter David Alfaro Siqueiros was then in Chile, painting the heroic murals of a school in the town of Chillán, which had been devastated by one of Chile's periodic earthquakes. He had been implicated in a Stalinist attempt on Trotsky's life in Mexico City and his commission to paint a mural in the Southern Cone was a kind of honorary exile. My father, as chargé d'affaires in Santiago, where his mission was to press the proudly independent Chileans to break relations with the Berlin–Rome Axis, rose above politics in the name of art and received Siqueiros regularly for lunch at the Mexican Embassy, which was a delirious mansion, worthy of William Beckford's follies, built by an enriched Italian tailor called Fallabella, on Santiago's broad Pedro de Valdivia Avenue.

This Gothic grotesque contained a Chinese room with nodding Buddhas, an office in what was known as Westminster Parliamentary style, Napoleonic lobbies, Louis XV dining rooms, Art Deco bedrooms, a Florentine loggia, many busts of Dante, and, finally, a vast Chilean vineyard in the back.

It was here, under the bulging Austral grapes, that I forced Siqueiros to sit after lunch and listen to me read our by then 400-page-long opus. As he drowsed off in the shade, I gained and lost my first reader. The novel, too, was lost; Torretti, who now teaches philosophy of science at the University of Puerto Rico, has no copy; Siqueiros is dead, and, besides, he slept right through my reading. I myself feel about it like Marlowe's Barabbas about fornication: that was in another country, and, besides, the wench is dead. Yet the experience of writing this highly imitative melodrama was not lost on me; its international setting, its self-conscious search for language (or languages, rather) were part of a constant attempt at a breakthrough in my life. My upbringing taught me that cultures are not isolated, and perish when deprived of contact with what is different and challenging. Reading, writing, teaching, learning, are all activities aimed at introducing civilizations to each other. No culture, I believed unconsciously ever since then, and quite consciously today, retains its identity in isolation; identity is attained in contact, in contrast, in breakthrough.

Rhetoric, said William Butler Yeats, is the language of our fight with others; poetry is the name of our fight with ourselves. My passage from English to Spanish determined the concrete expression of what, before, in Washington, had been the revelation of an identity. I wanted to write and I wanted to write in order to show myself that my identity and my country were real: now, in Chile, as I started to scribble my first stories, even publishing them in school magazines, I learned that I must in fact write in Spanish.

The English language, after all, did not need another writer. The English language has always been alive and kicking, and if it ever becomes drowsy, there will always be an Irishman . . .

In Chile I came to know the possibilities of our language for giving wing to freedom and poetry. The impression was enduring; it links me forever to that sad and wonderful land. It lives within me, and it transformed me into a man who knows how to dream, love, insult, and write only in Spanish. It also left me wide open to an incessant interrogation: What happened to this universal language, Spanish, which after the seventeenth century ceased to be a language of life, creation, dissatisfaction, and personal power and became far too often a language of mourning, sterility, rhetorical applause, and abstract power? Where were the threads of my tradition, where could I, writing in mid-twentieth century in Latin America, find the direct link to the great living presences I was then starting to read, my lost Cervantes, my old Quevedo, dead because he could not tolerate one more winter, my Góngora, abandoned in a gulf of loneliness?

At sixteen I finally went to live permanently in Mexico and there I found the answers to my quest for identity and language, in the thin air of a plateau of stone and dust that is the negative Indian image of another highland, that of central Spain. But, between Santiago and Mexico City, I spent six wonderful months in Argentina. They were, in spite of their brevity, so important in this reading and writing of myself that I must give them their full worth. Buenos Aires was then, as always, the most beautiful, sophisticated, and civilized city in Latin America, but in the summer of 1944, as street pavements melted in the heat and the city smelled of cheap wartime gasoline, rawhide from the port, and chocolate éclairs from the *confiterías,* Argentina had experienced a succession of military coups: General Rawson had overthrown President Castillo of the cattle oligarchy, but General Ramírez had then overthrown Rawson, and now General Farrell had overthrown Ramírez. A young colonel called Juan Domingo Perón was General Farrell's up-and-coming minister of Labor, and I heard an actress by the name of Eva Duarte play the "great women of history" on Radio Belgrano. A stultifying hack novelist who went by the pen name Hugo Wast was assigned to the Ministry of Education under his real name, Martínez Zuviría, and brought all his anti-Semitic, undemocratic, profascist phobias to the Buenos Aires high-school system, which I had suddenly been plunked into. Coming from the America of the New Deal, the ideals of revolutionary Mexico, and the politics of the Popular Front in Chile, I could not stomach this, rebelled, and was granted a full summer of wandering around Buenos Aires, free for the first time in my life, following my preferred tango orchestras – Canaro, D'Arienzo, and

Anibal Troilo, alias Pichuco – as they played all summer long in the Renoir-like shade and light of the rivers and pavilions of El Tigre and Maldonado. Now the comics were in Spanish: Mutt and Jeff were Benitín y Eneas. But Argentina had its own comic-book imperialism: through the magazines *Billiken* and *Patorozú,* all the children of Latin America knew from the crib that "las Malvinas son Argentinas."

Two very important things happened. First, I lost my virginity. We lived in an apartment building on the leafy corner of Callao and Quintana, and after 10 a.m. nobody was there except myself, an old and deaf Polish doorkeeper, and a beautiful Czech woman, aged thirty, whose husband was a film producer. I went up to ask her for her *Sintonía,* which was the radio guide of the forties, because I wanted to know when Evita was doing Joan of Arc. She said that had passed, but the next program was Madame Du Barry. I wondered if Madame Du Barry's life was as interesting as Joan of Arc's. She said it was certainly less saintly, and, besides, it could be emulated. How? I said innocently. And thereby my beautiful apprenticeship. We made each other very happy. And also very sad: this was not the liberty of love, but rather its libertine variety: we loved in hiding. I was too young to be a real sadist. So it had to end.

The other important thing was that I started reading Argentine literature, from the gaucho poems to Sarmiento's *Memories of Provincial Life* to Cané's *Juvenilia* to Güiraldes's *Don Segundo Sombra* to . . . to . . . to – and this was as good as discovering that Joan of Arc was also sexy – to Borges. I have never wanted to meet Borges personally because he belongs to that summer in B.A. He belongs to my personal discovery of Latin American literature.

II

Latin American extremes: if Cuba is the Andalusia of the New World, the Mexican plateau is its Castile. Parched and brown, inhabited by suspicious cats burnt too many times by foreign invasions, Mexico is the sacred zone of a secret hope: the gods shall return.

Mexican space is closed, jealous, and self-contained. In contrast, Argentine space is open and dependent on the foreign: migrations, exports, imports, words. Mexican space was vertically sacralized thousands of years ago. Argentine space patiently awaits its horizontal profanation.

I arrived on the Mexican highland from the Argentine pampa when I was sixteen years old. As I said, it was better to study in a country where the minister of Education was Jaime Torres Bodet than in a country where he was Hugo Wast. This was not the only contrast, or the most important one. A land isolated by its very nature – desert, mountain, chasm, sea, jungle, fire, ice, fugitive mists, and a sun that never blinks – Mexico is a multi-level temple that rises abruptly, blind to horizons, an arrow that wounds the sky but refuses the dangerous frontiers of the land, the canyons, the sierras without a human footprint, whereas the pampa is nothing if not an eternal frontier, the very portrait of the horizon, the sprawling flatland of a latent expansion awaiting, like a passive lover, the vast and rich overflow from that concentration of the transitory represented by the commercial metropolis of Buenos Aires, what Ezequiel Martínez Estrada called Goliath's head on David's body.

A well-read teenager, I had tasted the literary culture of Buenos Aires, then dominated by *Sur* magazine and Victoria Ocampo's enlightened mixture of the cattle oligarchy of the Pampas and the cultural clerisy of Paris, a sort of Argentinian cosmopolitanism. It then became important to appreciate the verbal differences between the Mexican culture, which, long before Paul Valéry, knew itself to be mortal, and the Argentine culture, founded on the optimism of powerful migratory currents from Europe, innocent of sacred stones or aboriginal promises. Mexico, closed to immigration by the TTT – the Tremendous Texas Trauma that in 1836 cured us once and for all of the temptation to receive Caucasian colonists because they had airport names like Houston and Austin and

Dallas – devoted its population to breeding like rabbits. Blessed by the Pope, Coatlicue, and Jorge Negrete, we are, all eighty million of us, Catholics in the Virgin Mary, misogynists in the stone goddesses, and *machistas* in the singing, pistol-packing *charro*.

The pampa goes on waiting: twenty-five million Argentinians today; scarcely five million more than in 1945, half of them in Buenos Aires.

Language in Mexico is ancient, old as the oldest dead. The eagles of the Indian empire fell, and it suffices to read the poems of the defeated to understand the vein of sadness that runs through Mexican literature, the feeling that words are identical to a farewell: "Where shall we go now, O my friends?" asks the Aztec poet of the Fall of Tenochtitlán: "The smoke lifts; the fog extends. Cry, my friends. Cry, oh cry." And the contemporary poet Xavier Villaurrutia, four centuries later, sings from the bed of the same lake, now dried up, from its dry stones:

In the midst of a silence deserted as a street before the crime
Without even breathing so that nothing may disturb my death
In this wall-less solitude
When the angels fled
In the grave of my bed I leave my bloodless statue.

A sad, underground language, forever being lost and recovered. I soon learned that Spanish as spoken in Mexico answered to six unwritten rules:

- Never use the familiar *tu* – thou – if you can use the formal you – *usted*.
- Never use the first-person possessive pronoun, but rather the second-person, as in "This is *your* home."
- Always use the first-person singular to refer to your own troubles, as in "Me fue del carajo, mano." But use the first-person plural when referring to your successes, as in "During our term, we distributed three million acres."

- Never use one diminutive if you can use five in a row.
- Never use the imperative when you can use the subjunctive.
- And only then, when you have exhausted these ceremonies of communication, bring out your verbal knife and plunge it deep into the other's heart: "Chinga a tu madre, cabrón."

The language of Mexicans springs from abysmal extremes of power and impotence, domination and resentment. It is the mirror of an overabundance of history, a history that devours itself before extinguishing and then regenerating itself, phoenix-like, once again. Argentina, on the contrary, is a tabula rasa, and it demands a passionate verbalization. I do not know another country that so fervently – with the fervor of Buenos Aires, Borges would say – opposes the silence of its infinite space, its physical and mental pampa, demanding: Please, *verbalize* me! Martin Fierro, Carlos Gardel, Jorge Luis Borges: reality must be captured, desperately, in the verbal web of the gaucho poem, the sentimental tango, the metaphysical tale: the pampa of the gaucho becomes the garden of the tango becomes the forked paths of literature.

What is forked? What is said.

What is said? What is forked.

Everything: Space. Time. Language. History. Our history. The history of Spanish America.

I read *Ficciones* as I flew north on a pontoon plane, courtesy of Pan American Airways. It was wartime, we had to have priority; all cameras were banned, and glazed plastic screens were put on our windows several minutes before we landed. Since I was not an Axis spy, I read Borges as we splashed into Santos, saying that the best proof that the Koran is an Arab book is that not a single camel is mentioned in its pages. I started thinking that the best proof that Borges is an Argentinian is in everything he has to evoke because it isn't there, as we glided into an invisible Rio de Janeiro. And as we flew out of Bahia, I thought that Borges invents a world because he needs it. I need, therefore I imagine.

By the time we landed in Trinidad, "Funes the Memorious"

and "Pierre Ménard, Author of Don Quixote" had introduced me, without my being aware, to the genealogy of the
serene madmen, the children of Erasmus. I did not know
then that this was the most illustrious family of modern fiction, since it went, backwards, from Pierre Ménard to Don
Quixote himself. During two short lulls in Santo Domingo
(then, horrifyingly, called Ciudad Trujillo) and Port-au-
Prince, I had been prepared by Borges to encounter my wonderful friends Toby Shandy, who reconstructs in his minia-
ture cabbage patch the battlefields of Flanders he was not able
to experience historically; Jane Austen's Catherine Moreland
and Gustave Flaubert's Madame Bovary, who like Don Quixote believe in what they read; Dickens's Mr. Micawber, who
takes his hopes to be realities; Dostoevsky's Myshkin, an idiot
because he gives the benefit of the doubt to the good possibility of mankind; Pérez Galdós's Nazarín, who is mad because
he believes that each human being can daily be Christ, and
who is truly St. Paul's madman: "Let him who seems wise
among you become mad, so that he might truly become wise."

   As we landed at Miami airport, the glazed windows disappeared once and for all and I knew that, like Pierre Ménard, a
writer must always face the mysterious duty of literally reconstructing a spontaneous work. And so I met my tradition: Don
Quixote was a book waiting to be written. The history of Latin
America was a history waiting to be lived.

                              III

When I finally arrived in Mexico, I discovered that my father's imaginary country was real, but more fantastic than any
imaginary land. It was as real as its physical and spiritual
borders: Mexico, the only frontier between the industrialized
and the developing worlds; the frontier between my country
and the United States, but also between all of Latin America
and the United States, and between the Catholic Mediterra-
nean and the Protestant Anglo-Saxon strains in the New
World.

It was with this experience and these questions that I approached the gold and mud of Mexico, the imaginary, imagined country, finally real but only real if I saw it from a distance that would assure me, because of the very fact of separation, that my desire for reunion with it would be forever urgent, and only real if I wrote it. Having attained some sort of perspective, I was finally able to write a few novels where I could speak of the scars of revolution, the nightmares of progress, and the perseverance of dreams.

I wrote with urgency because my absence became a destiny, yet a shared destiny: that of my own body as a young man, that of the old body of my country, and that of the problematic and insomniac body of my language. I could, perhaps, identify the former without too much trouble: Mexico and myself. But the language belonged to us all, to the vast community that writes and talks and thinks in Spanish. And without this language I could give no reality to either myself or my land. Language thus became the center of my personal being and of the possibility of forming my own destiny and that of my country into a shared destiny.

But nothing is shared in the abstract. Like bread and love, language and ideas are shared with human beings. My first contact with literature was sitting on the knees of Alfonso Reyes when the Mexican writer was ambassador to Brazil in the earlier thirties. Reyes had brought the Spanish classics back to life for us; he had written the most superb books on Greece; he was the most lucid of literary theoreticians; in fact, he had translated all of Western culture into Latin American terms. In the late forties, he was living in a little house the color of the *mamey* fruit, in Cuernavaca. He would invite me to spend weekends with him, and since I was eighteen and a night prowler, I kept him company from eleven in the morning, when Don Alfonso would sit in a café and toss verbal bouquets at the girls strolling around the plaza that was then a garden of laurels and not, as it has become, of cement. I do not know if the square, ruddy man seated at the next table was a British consul crushed by the nearness of the volcano;

but if Reyes, enjoying the spectacle of the world, quoted Lope de Vega and Garcilaso, our neighbor the *mescal* drinker would answer, without looking at us, with the more somber *stanze* of Marlowe and John Donne. Then we would go to the movies in order, Reyes said, to bathe in contemporary epic, and it was only at night that he would start scolding me: You have not read Stendhal yet? The world didn't start five minutes ago, you know.

He could irritate me. I read, against his classical tastes, the most modern, the most strident books, without understanding that I was learning his lesson: there is no creation without tradition; the "new" is an inflection on a preceding form; novelty is always a variation on the past. Borges said that Reyes wrote the best Spanish prose of our times. He taught me that culture had a smile, that the intellectual tradition of the whole world was ours by birthright, and that Mexican literature was important because it was literature, not because it was Mexican.

One day I got up very early (or maybe I came in very late from a binge) and saw him seated at five in the morning, working at his table, amid the aroma of the jacaranda and the bougainvillea. He was a diminutive Buddha, bald and pink, almost one of those elves who cobble shoes at night while the family sleeps. He liked to quote Goethe: Write at dawn, skim the cream of the day, then you can study crystals, intrigue at court, and make love to your kitchen maid. Writing in silence, Reyes did not smile. His world, in a way, ended on a funereal day in February 1913 when his insurrectionist father, General Bernardo Reyes, fell riddled by machine-gun bullets in the Zócalo in Mexico City, and with him fell what was left of Mexico's Belle Epoque, the long and cruel peace of Porfirio Díaz.

The smile of Alfonso Reyes had ashes on its lips. He had written, as a response to history, the great poem of exile and distance from Mexico: the poem of a cruel Iphigenia, the Mexican Iphigenia of the valley of Anáhuac:

I was another, being myself;
I was he who wanted to leave.
To return is to cry. I do not repent of this wide world.
It is not I who return,
But my shackled feet.

My father had remained in Buenos Aires as Mexican chargé d'affaires, with instructions to frown on Argentina's sympathies toward the Axis. My mother profited from his absence to enroll me in a Catholic school in Mexico City. The brothers who ruled this institution were preoccupied with something that had never entered my head: sin. At the start of the school year, one of the brothers would come before the class with a white lily in his hand and say: "This is a Catholic youth before kissing a girl." Then he would throw the flower on the floor, dance a little jig on it, pick up the bedraggled object, and confirm our worst suspicions: "This is a Catholic boy after . . ."

Well, all this made life very tempting. Retrospectively, I would agree with Luis Buñuel that sex without sin is like an egg without salt. The priests at the Colegio Francés made sex irresistible for us; they also made leftists of us by their constant denunciation of Mexican liberalism and especially of Benito Juárez. The sexual and political temptations became very great in a city where provincial mores and sharp social distinctions made it very difficult to have normal sexual relationships with young or even older women.

All this led, as I say, to a posture of rebellion that for me crystallized in the decision to be a writer. My father, by then back from Argentina, sternly said, Okay, go out and be a writer, but not at my expense. I became a very young journalist at the weekly *Siempre,* but my family pressured me to enter law school, or, in the desert of Mexican literature, I would literally die of hunger and thirst. I was sent to visit Alfonso Reyes in his enormous library-house, where he seemed more diminutive than ever, ensconced in a tiny corner he saved for his bed among the Piranesi-like perspective of volume piled upon volume. He said to me: "Mexico is a very formalistic country. If you don't have a title, you are nobody: *nadie, ninguno.* A title is like the handle on a cup; without it, no one will pick you up. You must become a *licenciado,* a lawyer; then you can do whatever you please, as I did."

So I entered the School of Law at the National University, where, as I feared, learning tended to be by rote. The budding explosion in the student population was compounded by cynical teachers who would spend the whole hour of class taking attendance on the two hundred students of civil law, from Aguilar to Zapata. But there were great exceptions of true teachers who understood that the law is inseparable from culture, from morality, and from justice. Foremost among these were the exiles from defeated Republican Spain, who enormously enriched Mexican universities, publishing houses, the arts, and the sciences. Don Manuel Pedroso, former dean of the University of Seville, made the study of law compatible with my literary inclinations. When I would bitterly complain about the dryness and boredom of learning the penal or mercantile codes by heart, he would counter: "Forget the codes. Read Dostoevsky, read Balzac. There's all you have to know about criminal or commercial law." He also made me see that Stendhal was right that the best model for a well-structured novel is the Napoleonic Code of Civil Law. Anyway, I found that culture consists of connections, not of separations: to specialize is to isolate.

Sex was another story, but Mexico City was then a manageable town of one million people, beautiful in its extremes of colonial and nineteenth-century elegance and the garishness of its exuberant and dangerous nightlife. My friends and I spent the last years of our adolescence and the first of our manhood in a succession of cantinas, brothels, strip joints, and silver-varnished nightclubs where the bolero was sung and the mambo danced; whores, mariachis, magicians were our companions as we struggled through our first readings of D. H. Lawrence and Aldous Huxley, James Joyce and André Gide, T. S. Eliot and Thomas Mann. Salvador Elizondo and I were the two would-be writers of the group, and if the realistic grain of *La Región Más Transparente (Where the Air Is Clear)* was sown in this, our rather somnambulistic immersion in the spectral nightlife of Mexico City, it is also true that the cruel imagination of an instant in Elizondo's *Farabeuf* had the same background experience. We would go to a whorehouse oddly called El Buen Tono, choose a poor Mexican girl who usually said her name was Gladys and she came from Guadalajara, and go to our respective rooms. One time, a horrible scream was heard and Gladys from Guadalajara rushed out, crying and streaming blood. Elizondo, in the climax of love, had slashed her armpit with a razor.

Another perspective, another distance for approximation, another possibility of sharing a language. In 1950 I went to Europe to do graduate work in international law at the University of Geneva. Octavio Paz had just published two books that had changed the face of Mexican literature, *Libertad Bajo Palabra* and *El Laberinto de la Soledad*. My friends and I had read those books aloud in Mexico, dazzled by a poetics that managed simultaneously to renew our language from within and to connect it to the language of the world.

At age thirty-six, Octavio Paz was not very different from what he is today. Writers born in 1914, like Paz and Julio Cortázar, surely signed a Faustian pact at the very mouth of hell's trenches; so many poets died in that war that someone had to take their place. I remember Paz in the so-called existentialist nightclubs of the time in Paris, in discussion with the very animated and handsome Albert Camus, who alternated philosophy and the boogie-woogie in La Rose Rouge. I remember Paz in front of the large windows of a gallery on the Place Vendôme, reflecting Max Ernst's great postwar painting "Europe after the Rain," and the painter's profile as an ancient eagle; and I tell myself that the poetics of Paz is an art of civilizations, a movement of encounters. Paz the poet meets Paz the thinker, because his poetry is a form of thought and his thought is a form of poetry; and as a result of this meeting, an encounter of civilizations takes place. Paz introduces civilizations to one another, makes them presentable before it is too late, because behind the wonderful smile of Camus, fixed forever in the absurdity of death, behind the bright erosion of painting by Max Ernst and the crystals of the Place Vendôme, Octavio and I, when we met, could hear the voice of *el poeta Libra,* Ezra, lamenting the death of the best, "for an old bitch gone in the teeth, for a botched civilization."

Octavio Paz has offered civilizations the mirror of their mortality, as Paul Valéry did, but also the reflection of their survival in an epidemic of meetings and erotic risks. In the generous friendship of Octavio Paz, I learned that there were no privileged centers of culture, race, or politics; that nothing should be left out of literature, because our time is a time of deadly reduction. The essential orphanhood of our time is seen in the poetry and thought of Paz as a challenge to be met through the renewed flux of human knowledge, of *all* human knowledge. We have not finished thinking, imagining, acting. It is still possible to know the world; we are unfinished men and women.

> I am not at the crossroads;
> > to choose
> is to go wrong.

For my generation in Mexico, the problem did not consist in discovering our modernity but in discovering our tradition. The latter was brutally denied by the comatose, petrified teaching of the classics in Mexican secondary schools: one had to bring Cervantes back to life in spite of a school system fatally oriented toward the ideal of universities as sausage factories; in spite of the more grotesque forms of Mexican nationalism of the time. A Marxist teacher once told me it was un-Mexican to read Kafka; a fascist critic said the same thing (this has been Kafka's Kafkian destiny everywhere), and a rather sterile Mexican author gave a pompous lecture at the Bellas Artes warning that readers who read Proust would proustitute themselves.

To be a writer in Mexico in the fifties, you had to be with

Alfonso Reyes and with Octavio Paz in the assertion that Mexico was not an isolated, virginal province but very much part of the human race and its cultural tradition; we were all, for good or evil, contemporary with all men and women.

In Geneva, I regained my perspective. I rented a garret overlooking the beautiful old square of the Bourg-du-Four, established by Julius Caesar as the Forum Boarium two millennia ago. The square was filled with coffeehouses and old bookstores. The girls came from all over the world; they were beautiful, and they were independent. When they were kissed, one did not become a sullied lily. We had salt on our lips. We loved each other, and I also loved going to the little island where the lake meets the river, to spend long hours reading. Since it was called Jean-Jacques Rousseau Island, I took along my volume of the *Confessions*. Many things came together then. A novel was the transformation of experience into history. The modern epic had been the epic of the first-person singular, of the I, from St. Augustine to Abélard to Dante to Rousseau to Stendhal to Proust. Joyce de-Joyced fiction: Here comes everybody! But H.C.E. did not collectively save the degraded Ego from exhaustion, self-doubt, and, finally, self-forgetfulness. When Odysseus says that he is nonexistent, we know and he knows that he is disguised; when Beckett's characters proclaim their nonbeing, we know that "the fact is notorious": they are no longer disguised. Kafka's man has been forgotten; no one can remember K the land surveyor; finally, as Milan Kundera tells us, nobody can remember Prague, Czechoslovakia, history.

I did not yet know this as I spent many reading hours on the little island of Rousseau at the intersection of Lake Geneva and the Rhône River back in 1951. But I vaguely felt that there was something beyond the exploration of the self that actually made the idea of human personality possible if the paths beyond it were explored. Cervantes taught us that a book is a book is a book: Don Quixote does not invite us into "reality" but into an act of the imagination where all things are real: the characters are active psychological entities, but also the archetypes they herald and always the figures from whence they come, which were unimaginable, unthinkable, like Don Quixote, before they became characters first and archetypes later.

Could I, a Mexican who had not yet written his first book, sitting on a bench on an early spring day as the *bise* from the Jura Mountains quieted down, have the courage to explore for myself, with my language, with my tradition, with my friends and influences, that region where the literary figure bids us consider it in the uncertainty of its gestation? Cervantes did it in a precise cultural situation: he brought into existence the modern world by having Don Quixote leave his secure village (a village whose name has been, let us remember, forgotten) and take to the open roads, the roads of the unsheltered, the unknown, and the different, there to lose what he read and to gain what we, the readers, read in him.

The novel is forever traveling Don Quixote's road, from the security of the analogous to the adventure of the different and even the unknown. In my way, this is the road I wanted to travel. I read Rousseau, or the adventures of the I; Joyce and Faulkner, or the adventures of the We; Cervantes, or the adventures of the You he calls the Idle, the Amiable Reader: you. And I read, in a shower of fire and in the lightning of enthusiasm, Rimbaud. His mother asked him what a particular poem was about. And he answered: "I have wanted to say what it says there, literally and in all other senses." This statement of Rimbaud's has been an inflexible rule for me and for what we are all writing today; and the present-day vigor of the literature of the Hispanic world, to which I belong, is not alien to this Rimbaudian approach to writing: Say what you mean, literally and in all other senses.

I think I imagined in Switzerland what I would try to write someday, but first I would have to do my apprenticeship. Only after many years would I be able to write what I then imagined; only years later, when I not only knew that I had the tools with which to do it, but also, and equally important, when I knew that if I did not write, death would not do it for

me. You start by writing to live. You end by writing so as not to
die. Love is the marriage of this desire and this fear. The
women I have loved I have desired for themselves, but also
because I feared myself.

IV

My first European experience came to a climax in the summer of 1950. It was a hot, calm evening on Lake Zurich, and
some wealthy Mexican friends had invited me to dinner at the
elegant Baur-au-Lac Hotel. The summer restaurant was a
floating terrace on the lake. You reached it by a gangplank,
and it was lighted by paper lanterns and flickering candles. As
I unfolded my stiff white napkin amid the soothing tinkle of
silver and glass, I raised my eyes and saw the group dining at
the next table.

Three ladies sat there with a man in his seventies. This man
was stiff and elegant, dressed in double-breasted white serge
and immaculate shirt and tie. His long, delicate fingers sliced
a cold pheasant, almost with daintiness. Yet even in eating he
seemed to me unbending, with a ramrod-back, military bearing. His aged face showed "a growing fatigue," but the pride
with which his lips and jaws were set sought desperately to
hide the fact, while the eyes twinkled with "the fiery play of
fancy."

As the carnival lights of that summer's night in Zurich
played with a fire of their own on the features I now recognized, Thomas Mann's face was a theater of implicit, quiet
emotions. He ate and let the ladies do the talking; he was, in
my fascinated eyes, a meeting place where solitude gives birth
to beauty unfamiliar and perilous, but also to the perverse
and the illicit. Thomas Mann had managed, out of this solitude, to find the affinity "between the personal destiny of
[the] author and that of his contemporaries in general."
Through him, I had imagined that the products of this solitude and of this affinity were named art (created by one) and

civilization (created by all). He spoke so surely, in *Death in Venice*, of the "tasks imposed upon him by his own ego and the European soul" that as I, paralyzed with admiration, saw him there that night I dared not conceive of such an affinity in our own Latin American culture, where the extreme demands of a ravaged, voiceless continent often killed the voice of the self and made a hollow political monster of the voice of the society, or killed it, giving birth to a pitiful, sentimental dwarf.

Yet, as I recalled my passionate reading of everything he wrote, from *Blood of the Walsungs* to *Dr. Faustus*, I could not help but feel that, in spite of the vast differences between his culture and ours, in both of them literature in the end asserted itself through a relationship between the visible and the invisible worlds of narration. A novel should "gather up the threads of many human destinies in the warp of a single idea"; the I, the You, and the We were only separate and dried up because of a lack of imagination. Unbeknownst to him, I left Thomas Mann sipping his demitasse as midnight approached and the floating restaurant bobbed slightly and the Chinese lanterns quietly flickered out. I shall always thank him for silently teaching me that, in literature, you know only what you imagine.

The Mexico of the forties and fifties I wrote about in *La Región Más Transparente* was an imagined Mexico, just as the Mexico of the eighties and nineties I am writing about in *Cristóbal Nonato (Christopher Unborn)* is totally imagined. I fear that we would know nothing of Balzac's Paris and Dickens's London if they, too, had not invented them. When in the spring of 1951 I took a Dutch steamer back to the New World, I had with me the ten Bible-paper tomes of the Pléiade edition of Balzac. This phrase of his has been a central creed of mine: "Wrest words from silence and ideas from obscurity." The reading of Balzac – one of the most thorough and metamorphosing experiences of my life as a novelist – taught me that one must exhaust reality, transcend it, in order to reach, to try to reach, that absolute which is made of the atoms of the relative: in Balzac, the marvelous words of *Séraphita* or *Louis Lambert* rest on the commonplace words of *Père Goriot* and *César Birotteau.* Likewise, the Mexican reality of *Where the Air Is Clear* and *The Death of Artemio Cruz* existed only to clash with my imagination, my negation, and my perversion of the facts, because, remember, I had learned to imagine Mexico before I ever knew Mexico.

This was, finally, a way of ceasing to tell what I understood and trying to tell, behind all the things I knew, the really important things: what I did not know. *Aura* illustrates this stance much too clearly, I suppose. I prefer to find it in a scene set in a cantina in *A Change of Skin,* or in a taxi drive in *The Hydra Head.* I never wanted to resolve an enigma, but to point out that there *was* an enigma.

I always tried to tell my critics: Don't classify me, read me. I'm a writer, not a genre. Do not look for the purity of the novel according to some nostalgic canon, do not ask for generic affiliation but rather for a dialogue, if not for the outright abolition, of genre; not for one language but for many languages at odds with one another; not, as Bakhtin would put it, for unity of style but for *heteroglossia,* not for monologic but for dialogic imagination. I'm afraid that, by and large, in Mexico at least, I failed in this enterprise. Yet I am not disturbed by this fact, because of what I have just said: language is a shared and sharing part of culture that cares little about formal classifications and much about vitality and connection, for culture itself perishes in purity or isolation, which is the deadly wages of perfection. Like bread and love, language is shared with others. And human beings share a tradition. There is no creation without tradition. No one creates from nothing.

I went back to Mexico, but knew that I would forever be a wanderer in search of perspective: this was my real baptism, not the religious or civil ceremonies I have mentioned. But no matter where I went, Spanish would be the language of my writing and Latin America the culture of my language.

Neruda, Reyes, Paz; Washington, Santiago de Chile, Buenos Aires, Mexico City, Paris, Geneva; Cervantes, Balzac, Rimbaud, Thomas Mann: only with all the shared languages, those of my places and friends and masters, was I able to approach the fire of literature and ask it for a few sparks.

EDUARDO GALEANO

In Defense of the Word:
Leaving Buenos Aires, June 1976

1

One writes out of a need to communicate and to commune
with others, to denounce that which gives pain and to share
that which gives happiness. One writes against one's solitude
and against the solitude of others. One assumes that literature
transmits knowledge and affects the behavior and language
of those who read, thus helping us to know ourselves better
and to save ourselves collectively. But "others" is too vague;
and in times of crisis, times of definition, ambiguities may too
closely resemble lies. One writes, in reality, for the people
whose luck or misfortune one identifies with – the hungry, the
sleepless, the rebels, and the wretched of this earth – and the
majority of them are illiterate. Among the literate minority,
how many can afford to buy books? Is this contradiction resolved by proclaiming that one writes for that facile abstrac-
tion known as "the masses"?

2

We were not born on the moon, we don't live in seventh
heaven. We have the good fortune and the misfortune to

belong to a tormented region of the world, Latin America, and to live in a historic period that is relentlessly oppressive. The contradictions of class society are sharper here than in the rich countries. Massive misery is the price paid by the poor countries so that 6 percent of the world's population may consume with impunity half the wealth generated by the entire world. The abyss, the distance between the well-being of some and the misery of others, is greater in Latin America; and the methods necessary to maintain this distance are more savage.

The development of a restrictive and dependent industry, which was superimposed on the old agrarian and mining structures without changing the latter's essential distortions, has sharpened social contradictions rather than alleviating them. The skills of the traditional politicians – experts in the arts of seduction and swindling – are today inadequate, antiquated, useless. The populist game which granted concessions – the better to manipulate – is no longer possible in some cases, and in others it reveals its dangerous double edge. Thus the dominant classes and countries resort to their repressive apparatuses. How else could a social system survive which more and more resembles a concentration camp? How, without barbed-wire fences, keep within bounds the growing legion of the damned? To the extent that the system finds itself threatened by the relentless growth of unemployment, poverty, and the resultant social and political tensions, room for pretense and good manners shrinks: in the outskirts of the world the system reveals its true face.

Why not recognize a certain sincerity in the dictatorships that today oppress the majority of our countries? Freedom of enterprise means, in times of crisis, the deprivation of freedom for people. Latin American scientists emigrate, laboratories and universities have no funds, industrial "know-how" is always foreign and exorbitantly expensive; but why not recognize a certain creativity in the development of a technology of terror? Latin America is making inspired universal contributions to the development of methods of torture, techniques for assassinating people and ideas, for the cultivation of silence, the extension of impotence, and the sowing of fear.

How can those of us who want to work for a literature that helps to make audible the voice of the voiceless function in the context of this reality? Can we make ourselves heard in the midst of a deaf-mute culture? The small freedom conceded to writers, is it not at times a proof of our failure? How far can we go? Whom can we reach?

A noble task, that of heralding the world of the just and the free; a noble function, that of rejecting a system of hunger and of cages – visible and invisible. But how many yards to the border? How long will those in power continue to give us their permission?

3

There has been much discussion of direct forms of censorship imposed by diverse sociopolitical regimes, of the prohibition of books or newspapers that are embarrassing or dangerous to them, and the exile, imprisonment, or murder of writers and journalists. But indirect censorship functions more subtly; it is no less real for being less apparent. Little is said about it, yet it is what most profoundly defines the oppressive and excluding character of the system to which most Latin American countries are subjected. What is the nature of this censorship which does not declare itself? It resides in the fact that the boat does not sail because there is no water in the sea; if only 5 percent of the Latin American population can buy refrigerators, what percentage can buy books? And what percentage can read them, feel a need for them, absorb their influence?

Latin American writers, wage workers in a cultural industry which serves the consumption needs of an enlightened elite, come from, and write for, a minority. This is the objective situation of both those writers whose work condones social inequity and the dominant ideology and those who attempt to break with it. We are, to a large extent, blocked by the game rules of the reality in which we function.

The prevailing social order perverts or annihilates the creative capacity of the immense majority of people and reduces the possibility of creation – an age-old response to human anguish and the certainty of death – to its professional exercise by a handful of specialists. How many "specialists" are we in Latin America? For whom do we write, whom do we reach? Where is our real public? (Let us mistrust applause. At times we are congratulated by those who consider us innocuous.)

4

One writes in order to deflect death and strangle the specters that haunt us; but what one writes can be historically useful only when in some way it coincides with the need of the collectivity to achieve its identity. This, I think, is what one wants. In saying: "This is who I am," in revealing oneself, the writer can help others to become aware of who they are. As a means of revealing collective identity, art should be considered an article of prime necessity, not a luxury. But in Latin America access to the products of art and culture is forbidden to the immense majority.

For the peoples whose identity has been shattered by the successive cultures of conquest, and whose merciless exploitation contributes to the functioning of the machinery of world capitalism, the system generates a "mass culture." Culture *for* the masses is a more precise description of this degraded art of the mass media, which manipulates consciousness, conceals reality, and stifles the creative imagination. Naturally it does not lead to a revelation of identity but is rather a means of erasing or distorting it in order to impose ways of life and patterns of consumption which are widely disseminated through the mass media. The culture of the dominant class is called "national culture"; it lives an imported life and limits itself to imitating, stupidly and vulgarly, so-called universal culture – or that which passes for such among those who confuse it with the culture of the dominant countries. In our time, an era of multiple markets and multinational corporations, both economics and culture (that is, "mass culture") have been internationalized, thanks to accelerated development and the mass media. The centers of power export not only machinery and patents to us, but also ideology. If in Latin America the enjoyment of worldly goods is limited to the few, it then follows that the majority must resign itself to the consumption of fantasy. Illusions of wealth are sold to the poor, illusions of freedom to the oppressed, dreams of victory to the defeated and of power to the weak. One need not be literate to consume the inviting symbols presented by television, radio, and films in their effort to justify the unequal organization of the world.

In order to maintain the status quo in these lands, where each minute a child dies of disease or hunger, we must look at ourselves through the eyes of those who oppress us. People are trained to accept *this* order as *natural,* therefore eternal; and the system is identified with the fatherland, so that an enemy of the regime is by extension a traitor or a foreign agent. The law of the jungle, which is the law of the system, is sanctified, so that the defeated peoples will accept their condition as destiny; by falsifying the past, the true causes of Latin America's historical failure are passed over – Latin America, whose poverty has always fed alien wealth. On the small television screen and on the large, the best man wins, the best being the strongest. The waste, the exhibitionism, and the unscrupulousness produce not revulsion but admiration; everything can be bought, sold, rented, consumed, including the soul. Magical properties are attributed to a cigarette, a car, a bottle of whiskey, or a wristwatch: they can provide us with personalities, they can guide us toward success and happiness. The proliferation of foreign heroes and role models parallels the fetishism of brand names and fashions of the rich countries. The local *fotonovelas** and soap operas take

* Translator's Note: A *fotonovela* is a story of the True Romances genre, presented in comic book form, illustrated with photographs in place of cartoons.

place in a limbo of pretentiousness, peripheral to the real social and political problems of each country; and the imported serials sell Western, Christian democracy together with violence and tomato sauce.

5

In these lands of young people – young people whose numbers grow incessantly and who find no employment – the tick-tock of the time bomb obliges those who rule to sleep with one eye open. The multiple methods of cultural alienation – mechanisms used to drug and to castrate – take on increasing importance. The formulas for the sterilization of consciousness are put into practice with greater success than those for birth control.

The best way to colonize consciousness is to suppress it. In this sense also, the importation, whether deliberate or not, of a false counterculture, which finds a growing echo in the rising generations of some Latin American countries, plays a role. Those countries which do not offer the option of political participation – because of the fossilization of their structures or because of their stifling mechanisms of repression – offer the most fertile ground for the proliferation of a so-called culture of protest, originating outside the country, a sub-product of the leisure and waste which is focused on all social classes and originates in the spurious anticonventionalism of the parasite classes.

The customs and symbols of the resurgent youth of the sixties in the United States and Europe, born of a reaction against the uniformity of consumption, have become objects of assembly-line production in Latin America. Clothing with psychedelic designs is sold, accompanied by exhortations to "free yourself"; music, posters, hair styles, and clothing that reproduce the esthetic models of drug hallucination become mass-market items for the Third World. Together with the symbols, colorful and appealing as they are, tickets to limbo are offered to young people who are attempting to flee the inferno. The new generations are invited to abandon a history which is painful for a trip to Nirvana. By joining this "drug culture" certain young Latin Americans achieve the illusion of reproducing the lifestyle of their metropolitan counterparts.

Originating in the lack of conformity of marginal groups in industrial alienated society, this false counterculture has nothing to do with our real needs of identity and destiny; it provides adventures for the immobilized; it generates resignation, egotism, noncommunication; it leaves reality intact but changes its image; it promises painless love and warless peace. Furthermore, by converting sensations into consumer goods, it dovetails perfectly with the "supermarket ideology" disseminated by the mass media. If the fetishism of cars and refrigerators is not sufficient to mute anguish and to calm anxieties, it is at least possible to buy peace, intensity, and happiness in the underground supermarket.

6

To awaken consciousness, to reveal reality – can literature claim a better function in these times and in these lands of ours? The culture of the system, the culture of reality-substitutes, disguises reality and anesthetizes consciousness. But what can a writer do – however much his or her flame burns – against the ideological mechanisms of lies and conformism?

If society tends to organize itself in such a way that contact between humans is precluded, and human relations are reduced to a sinister game of competition and consumption – of isolated individuals using and abusing each other – what role can be played by a literature of fraternal ties and collective solidarity? We have reached a point where to name things is to denounce them: but, to whom and for whom?

7

Our own fate as Latin American writers is linked to the need for profound social transformations. To narrate is to give oneself: it seems obvious that literature, as an effort to communicate fully, will continue to be blocked from the start, so

long as misery and illiteracy exist, and so long as the posses-
sors of power continue to carry out with impunity their policy
of collective imbecilization, through the instruments of the
mass media.

I don't share the attitude of those who demand special
freedom for writers, independently of freedom for other
workers. Great changes, deep structural changes, will be necessary in our countries if we writers are to go beyond the
citadels of the elites, if we are to express ourselves, free of
visible and invisible restraints. In an incarcerated society, free
literature can exist only as denunciation and hope.

At the same time, I think that it would be a midsummer
night's dream to imagine that the creative potential of the
people could be realized through cultural means alone – the
people, who were lulled to sleep long ago by harsh conditions
of existence and the exigencies of life. How many talents have
been extinguished in Latin America before they could reveal
themselves? How many writers and artists have never had the
opportunity to recognize themselves as such?

8

Furthermore, can a national culture be achieved completely
in countries where the material bases of power are not indigenous but are dependent on foreign metropoli?

This being the case, does it make sense to write? There is no
"degree zero" of culture, just as there is no "degree zero" of
history. If we recognize an inevitable continuity between the
stage of domination and the stage of liberation in any process
of social development, why negate the importance of literature and its possible revolutionary role in the exploration,
revelation, and diffusion of our real and potential identity?
The oppressor does not want the mirror to reflect anything to
the oppressed but its quicksilver surface. What process of
change can activate a people that doesn't know who it is, nor
from whence it comes? If it doesn't know who it is, how can it

know what it deserves to become? Cannot literature aid, directly or indirectly, in this revelation?

It seems to me that the possibility of contribution depends to a large extent on the level of intensity of the writer's responsiveness to his or her people – their roots, their vicissitudes, their destiny – and the ability to perceive the heartbeat, the sound and rhythm, of the authentic counterculture, which is on the rise. That which is considered "uncultured" often contains the seeds or fruits of *another* culture, which confronts the dominant one and does not share its values or its rhetoric. It is frequently and erroneously dismissed as a mere degraded imitation of the "culture products" of the elite or of the cultural models turned out by the system on an assembly-line basis. But a popular narrative is oftentimes more revealing and more meaningful than a "professional" novel, and the pulse of life is conveyed more forcefully in certain anonymous folksong couplets than in many volumes of poetry written in the code of the initiated. The testimonies of the people as they express in a thousand ways their tribulations and their hopes are more eloquent and beautiful than the books written "in the name of the people."

Our authentic collective identity is born out of the past and is nourished by it – our feet tread where others trod before us; the steps we take were prefigured – but this identity is not frozen into nostalgia. We are not, to be sure, going to discover our hidden countenance in the artificial perpetuation of customs, clothing, and curios which tourists demand of conquered peoples. *We are what we do, especially what we do to change what we are*: our identity resides in action and in struggle. Therefore, the revelation of what we are implies the denunciation of those who stop us from being what we can become. In defining ourselves our point of departure is challenge, and struggle against obstacles.

A literature born in the process of crisis and change, and deeply immersed in the risks and events of its time, can indeed help to create the symbols of the new reality, and perhaps – if talent and courage are not lacking – throw light on the signs along the road. It is not futile to sing the pain and the beauty of having been born in America.

9

Neither press runs nor sales figures necessarily provide a valid measure of the impact of a book. At times the written work radiates an influence much greater than is apparent; at times, it answers – years in advance – the questions and needs of the collectivity, if the writer has known how to experience them first, through inner doubts and agonies. Writing springs from the wounded consciousness of the writer and is projected onto the world; the act of creation is an act of solidarity which does not always fulfill its destiny during the lifetime of its creator.

10

I do not share the attitude of those writers who claim for themselves divine privileges not granted to ordinary mortals, nor of those who beat their breasts and rend their clothes as they clamor for public pardon for having lived a life devoted to serving a useless vocation. Neither so godly, nor so contemptible. Awareness of our limitations does not imply impotence: literature, a form of action, is not invested with supernatural powers, but the writer may become something of a magician if he or she procures, through a literary work, the survival of significant experiences and individuals.

If what is written is read seriously and to some extent changes or nourishes the consciousness of the reader, a writer has justified his or her role in the process of change: with neither arrogance nor false humility, but with the recognition of being a small part of something vast.

It seems to me appropriate that those who reject the word are the ones who cultivate monologues with their own shadows and with their endless labyrinths; but the word has significance for those of us who wish to celebrate and share the certainty that the human condition is not a cesspool. We seek interlocutors, not admirers; we offer dialogue, not spectacle. Our writing is informed by a desire to make contact, so that readers may become involved with words that came to us from others, and that return to them as hope and prophecy.

11

To claim that literature on its own is going to change reality would be an act of madness or arrogance. It seems to me no less foolish to deny that it can aid in making this change. The awareness of our limitations is undoubtedly an awareness of our reality. Amidst the fog of desperation and doubt, it is possible to face it and wrestle with it – with our limitations, but at the same time in opposition to them.

In this respect a "revolutionary" literature written for the convinced is just as much an abandonment as is a conservative literature devoted to the ecstatic contemplation of one's own navel. There are those who cultivate an "ultra" literature of apocalyptic tone, addressed to a limited public, convinced beforehand of what it proposes and transmits. What risk do these writers run, however revolutionary they claim to be, if they write for the minority that thinks and feels as they do, and if they give that minority what it expects? In such cases there is no possibility of failure; neither is there a possibility of success. What is the use of writing, if not to challenge the blockade imposed by the system on the dissenting message?

Our effectiveness depends on our capacity to be audacious and astute, clear and appealing. I would hope that we can create a language more fearless and beautiful than that used by conformist writers to greet the twilight.

12

But it is not only a problem of language; it is also one of media. The culture of resistance employs all the means available to it, and does not grant itself the luxury of wasting any vehicle or opportunity of expression. Time is short, the challenge a burning one, the task enormous; for a Latin American writer, enlisted in the cause of social change, the production of books constitutes one sector on a front of multiple efforts. We do not share the sanctification of literature as a frozen institution of bourgeois culture. Mass-market narrative and reportage, television, film, and radio scripts, popular songs are not always minor "genres" of inferior character, as is claimed by certain lords of specialized literary discourse, who look down on them. The fissures opened by Latin American rebel journalism in the alienating mechanisms of the mass media have frequently been the result of dedicated and creative works, which need no apology for their esthetic level or their efficacy when compared with good novels and short stories.

13

I believe in my vocation; I believe in my instrument. I cannot understand why those writers write who declare airily that writing makes no sense in a world where people are dying of hunger. Nor can I understand those who convert the word into the target of their rage and into a fetish. Words are weapons, and they can be used for good or for evil; the crime can never be blamed on the knife.

I think that a primordial function of Latin American literature today is the rescue of the word, frequently used and abused with impunity for the purpose of hampering and betraying communication.

"Freedom" in my country is the name of a jail for political prisoners, and "democracy" forms part of the title of various regimes of terror; the word "love" defines the relationship of a man with his automobile, and "revolution" is understood to describe what a new detergent can do in your kitchen; "glory" is something that a certain smooth soap produces in its user, and "happiness" is a sensation experienced while eating hot dogs. "A peaceful country" means, in many countries of Latin America, "a well-kept cemetery," and sometimes "healthy man" must be read as "impotent man."

By writing it is possible to offer, in spite of persecution and censorship, the testimony of our time and our people – for now and for later. One may write as if to say: "We are here, we were here; we are thus, we were thus." In Latin America a literature is taking shape and acquiring strength, a literature that does not lull its readers to sleep, but rather awakens them; that does not propose to bury our dead, but to immortalize them; that refuses to stir the ashes but rather attempts to light the fire. This literature perpetuates and enriches a powerful tradition of combative words. If, as we believe, hope is preferable to nostalgia, perhaps that nascent literature may come to deserve the beauty of the social forces which, sooner or later, by hook or by crook, will radically alter the course of our history. And perhaps it may help to preserve for the generations to come – in the words of the poet – "the true name of all things."

Translated by Bobbye S. Ortiz

GUILLERMO GÓMEZ-PEÑA

Documented/Undocumented

I live smack in the fissure between two worlds, in the infected wound: half a block from the end of Western Civilization and four miles from the start of the Mexican–American border, the northernmost point of Latin America. In my fractured reality, but a reality nonetheless, there cohabit two histories, languages, cosmologies, artistic traditions, and political systems which are drastically counterposed. Many "deterritorialized" Latin American artists in Europe and the U.S. have opted for "internationalism" (a cultural identity based upon the "most advanced" of the ideas originating out of New York or Paris). I, on the other hand, opt for "borderness" and assume my role: My generation, the *chilangos* [slang term for a Mexico City native], who came to "el norte" fleeing the imminent ecological and social catastrophe of Mexico City, gradually integrated itself into otherness, in search of that other Mexico grafted onto the entrails of the et cetera... became Chicano-ized. We de-Mexicanized ourselves to Mexi-understand ourselves, some without wanting to, others on purpose. And one day, the border became our house, laboratory, and ministry of culture (or counterculture).

Today, eight years after my departure [from Mexico], when they ask me for my nationality or ethnic identity, I can't respond with one word, since my "identity" now possesses multiple repertories: I am Mexican but I am also Chicano and Latin American. At the border they call me *chilango* or *mexi-quillo*; in Mexico City it's *pocho* or *norteño*; and in Europe it's *sudaca*. The Anglos call me "Hispanic" or "Latino," and the Germans have, on more than one occasion, confused me with Turks or Italians. My wife Emilia is Anglo-Italian, but speaks Spanish with an Argentine accent, and together we walk amid the rubble of the Tower of Babel of our American post-modernity.

The recapitulation of my personal and collective topography has become my cultural obsession since I arrived in the United States. I look for the traces of my generation, whose distance stretches not only from Mexico City to California, but also from the past to the future, from pre-Columbian America to high technology and from Spanish to English, passing through "Spanglish."

As a result of this process I have become a cultural topographer, border-crosser, and hunter of myths. And it doesn't matter where I find myself, in Califas or Mexico City, in Barcelona or West Berlin; I always have the sensation that I belong to the same species: the migrant tribe of fiery pupils.

My work, like that of many border artists, comes from two distinct traditions, and because of this has dual, or on occasion multiple, referential codes. One strain comes from Mexican popular culture, the Latin American literary "boom," and the Mexico City counterculture of the '70s . . . the other comes directly from fluxus (a late-'60s international art movement that explored alternative means of production and distribution), concrete poetry, conceptual art, and performance art. These two traditions converge in my border experience and they fuse together.

In my intellectual formation, Carlos Fuentes, Gabriel García Márquez, Oscar Chávez, Felipe Ehrenberg, José Agustín, and Enrique Cisneros were as important as Burroughs, Foucault, Fassbinder, Lacan, Vito Aconci, and Joseph Beuys.

My "artistic space" is the intersection where the new Mexican

urban poetry and the colloquial Anglo poetry meet; the intermediate stage somewhere between Mexican street theater and
multimedia performance; the silence that snaps in between
the *corrido* and punk; the wall that divides *"neográfica"* (a
1970s Mexico City art movement involved in the production
of low-budget book art and graphics) and graffiti; the high-
way that joins Mexico City and Los Angeles; and the mysterious thread of thought and action that puts pan–Latin
Americanism in touch with the Chicano movement, and both
of these in touch with other international vanguards.

I am a child of crisis and cultural syncretism, half hippie
and half punk. My generation grew up watching movies
about cowboys and science fiction, listening to *cumbias* and
tunes from the Moody Blues, constructing altars and filming
in Super-8, reading the *Corno Emplumado* and *Artforum,* traveling to Tepoztlán and San Francisco, creating and de-creating
myths. We went to Cuba in search of political illumination, to
Spain to visit the crazy grandmother and to the U.S. in search
of the instantaneous musico-sexual Paradise. We found nothing. Our dreams wound up getting caught in the webs of the
border.

Our generation belongs to the world's biggest floating population: the weary travelers, the dislocated, those of us who
left because we didn't fit anymore, those of us who still haven't
arrived because we don't know where to arrive at, or because
we can't go back anymore.

Our deepest generational emotion is that of loss, which
comes from our having left. Our loss is total and occurs at
multiple levels: loss of our country (culture and national rit-
uals) and our class (the "illustrious" middle class and upper
middle). Progressive loss of language and literary culture in
our native tongue (those of us who live in non-Spanish-speak-
ing countries); loss of ideological meta-horizons (the repression against and division of the left) and of metaphysical
certainty.

In exchange, what we won was a vision of a more experi-
mental culture, that is to say, a multi-focal and tolerant one.

Going beyond nationalisms, we established cultural alliances with other places, and we won a true political conscience (declassicization and consequent politicization) as well as new options in social, sexual, spiritual, and aesthetic behavior.

Our artistic product presents hybrid realities and colliding visions within coalition. We practice the epistemology of multiplicity and a border semiotics. We share certain thematic interests, like the continual clash with cultural otherness, the crisis of identity, or, better said, access to trans- or multiculturalism, and the destruction of borders therefrom; the creation of alternative cartographies, a ferocious critique of the dominant culture of both countries, and, lastly, a proposal for new creative languages.

We witness the borderization of the world, by-product of the "deterritorialization" of vast human sectors. The borders either expand or are shot full of holes. Cultures and languages mutually invade one another. The South rises and melts, while the North descends dangerously with its economic and military pincers. The East moves west and vice-versa. Europe and North America daily receive uncontainable migrations of human beings, a majority of whom are being displaced involuntarily. This phenomenon is the result of multiple factors: regional wars, unemployment, overpopulation, and especially in the enormous disparity in North/South relations.

The demographic facts are staggering: The Middle East and Black Africa are already in Europe, and Latin America's heart now beats in the U.S. New York and Paris increasingly resemble Mexico City and São Paulo. Cities like Tijuana and Los Angeles, once socio-urban aberrations, are becoming models of a new hybrid culture, full of uncertainty and vitality. And border youth – the fearsome "cholo-punks," children of the chasm that is opening between the "first" and the "third" worlds, become the indisputable heirs to a new *mestizaje* (the fusion of the Amerindian and European races).

In this context, concepts like "high culture," "ethnic purity," "cultural identity," "beauty," and "fine arts" are absurdities and anachronisms. Like it or not, we are attending the funeral of modernity and the birth of a new culture.

In 1988, the unigeneric and monocultural vision of the world is insufficient. Syncretism, interdisciplinarianism, and multi-ethnicity are sine qua nons of contemporary art. And the artist or intellectual who doesn't comprehend this will be banished and his or her work will not form part of the great cultural debates of the continent.

Art is conceptual territory where everything is possible, and by the same token there do not exist certainties nor limitations within it. In 1988, all the creative possibilities have been explored, and therefore they are all within our reach.

Thanks to the discoveries and advancements of many artists over the last fifteen years, the concept of *metier* is so wide and the parameters of art so flexible that they include practically every imaginable alternative: art as political negotiation (Felipe Ehrenberg – Mexico), as social reform (Joseph Beuys – Germany), as an instrument of multicultural organization (Judy Baca – Los Angeles), or as alternative communication (*Post Arte* – Mexico, and Kit Galloway & Sherri Rabinowitz – USA). Others conceive art as a strategy of intervention aimed at mass media, or as citizen-diplomacy, social chronicle, a popular semiotics, or personal anthropology.

In 1988, our artistic options in terms of the medium, methodology, system of communication, and channels of distribution for our ideas and images are greater and more diverse than ever. Not understanding and practicing this freedom implies operating outside of history, or, worse yet, blindly accepting the restrictions imposed by cultural bureaucracies.

Our experience as Latino border artists and intellectuals in the U.S. fluctuates between legality and illegality, between partial citizenship and full. For the Anglo community we are simply "an ethnic minority," a subculture, that is to say, some kind of pre-industrial tribe with a good consumerist appetite. For the art world, we are practitioners of distant languages that, in the best of cases, are perceived as exotic.

In general, we are perceived through the folkloric prisms of Hollywood, fad literature and publicity; or through the ideological filters of mass media. For the average Anglo, we are nothing but "images," "symbols," "metaphors." We lack ontological existence and anthropological concreteness. We are perceived indistinctly as magic creatures with shamanistic powers, happy bohemians with pretechnological sensibilities, or as romantic revolutionaries born in a Cuban poster from the '70s. All this without mentioning the more ordinary myths, which link us with drugs, supersexuality, gratuitous violence, and terrorism, myths that serve to justify racism and disguise the fear of cultural otherness.

These mechanisms of mythification generate semantic interference and obstruct true intercultural dialogue. To make border art implies to reveal and subvert said mechanisms.

The term Hispanic, coined by techno-marketing experts and by the designers of political campaigns, homogenizes our cultural diversity (Chicanos, Cubans, and Puerto Ricans become indistinguishable), avoids our indigenous cultural heritage and links us directly with Spain. Worse yet, it possesses connotations of upward mobility and political obediance.

The terms *Third World culture, ethnic art,* and *minority art* are openly ethnocentric and necessarily imply an axiological vision of the world at the service of Anglo-European culture. Confronted with them, one can't avoid asking the following questions: Besides possessing more money and arms, is it that the "First World" is qualitatively better in any other way than our "underdeveloped" countries? That the Anglos themselves aren't also an "ethnic group," one of the most violent and antisocial tribes on this planet? That the five hundred million Latin American *mestizos* that inhabit the Americas are a "minority"?

Between Chicanos, Mexicans, and Anglos there is a heritage of relations poisoned by distrust and resentment. For this reason, my cultural work (especially in the camps of performance art and journalism) has concentrated itself upon the destruction of the myths and the stereotypes that each group has invented to rationalize the other two.

With the dismantling of this mythology, I look, if not to create an instantaneous space for intercultural communication, at least to contribute to the creation of the groundwork and theoretical principles for a future dialogue that is capable of transcending the profound historical resentments that exist between the communities on either side of the border.

Within the framework of the false amnesty of the Immigration Reform and Control Act and the growing influence of the North American ultra-right, which seeks to close (militarize) the border because of supposed motives of "national security," the collaboration among Chicano, Mexican, and Anglo artists has become indispensable.

Anglo artists can contribute their technical ability, their comprehension of the new mediums of expression and information (video and audio), and their altruist/internationalist tendencies. In turn, Latinos (whether Mexican, Chicano, Caribbean, Central or South American) can contribute the originality of their cultural models, their spiritual strength, and their political understanding of the world.

Together, we can collaborate in surprising cultural projects but without forgetting that *both should retain control of the product,* from the planning stages up through to distribution. If this doesn't occur, then intercultural collaboration isn't authentic. We shouldn't confuse true collaboration with political paternalism, cultural vampirism, voyeurism, economic opportunism, and demogogic multiculturalism.

We should clear up this matter once and for all:

We (Latinos in the United States) don't want to be a mere ingredient of the melting pot. What we want is to participate actively in a humanistic, pluralistic and politicized dialogue, continuous and not sporadic, and that this occur between equals that enjoy the same power of negotiation.

For this "intermediate space" to open, first there has to be a pact of mutual cultural understanding and acceptance, and it is precisely in this that the border artist can contribute. In this very delicate historical moment, Mexican artists and intellectuals as well as Chicanos and Anglos should try to "recontextualize" ourselves, that is to say, search for a "common cultural territory," and within it put into practice new models of communication and association.

Translated by Rubén Martínez

DAVID MURA

Strangers in the Village

Recently, in *The Village Voice,* a number of articles were devoted to the issue of race in America. Perhaps the most striking
article, "Black Women, White Kids: A Tale of Two Worlds,"
was about Black women in New York City who take care of
upper-middle-class and upper-class white children. Merely by
describing the situation of these Black women and recording
their words, the article pointed out how race and class affects
these women's lives: "As the nanny sits in the park watching a
tow-haired child play, her own kids are coming home from
school; they will do their homework alone and make dinner."

None of the white people who employed these nannies
seemed at all cognizant of the contradictions of this description. Instead the whites seemed to view the Black nannies as a
natural facet of their lives, an expected privilege. Yet, on another less-conscious level, the whites appeared to have misgiv-
ings that they could not express. One of the nannies, named
Bertha, talked about how she objected to the tone of voice her
employer, Barbra, used: "You wait a minute here, Barbra. I'm
not a child," Bertha would tell Barbra, "I can talk to you any
way I want. This is a free country, it's not a commie country."
Every time Bertha and Barbra have an argument, Barbra
buys Bertha presents: "She bought me shoes, a beautiful
blouse, a Mother's Day present... she's a very generous

person. She's got a good heart." But Bertha doesn't really like the presents. "It always made me feel guilty. To tell you the truth about it, I never had too many people give me presents, so it just made me feel bad.

"Another reason we don't get along," Bertha continues, "is she always trying to figure me out. See, I'm a very complicated person. I'm a very moody person . . . I'm independent. I figure I can deal with it myself. And we would sit there, I could just feel her eyes on me, and I'd have to get up and leave the room . . . She just wants you to be satisfied with her all the time . . . She wants me to tell her I love you. I just can't."

The author of the article says that sometimes Barbra seems to want love and sometimes she seems to want forgiveness. "But perhaps for most white people, a black person's affection can never mean more than an act of absolution for historical and collective guilt, an affection desired not because of how one feels about that particular person but because that person is black."

As a middle-class third-generation Japanese-American, I read this article with mixed feelings. On one level, I have much more in common with Bertha's employer, Barbra, than I do with Bertha. Although at one time Japanese-Americans worked in jobs similar to Bertha's and were part of the lower class, by my generation this was not the case. I grew up in the suburbs of Chicago, went to college and graduate school, married a pediatrician who is three-quarters WASP and one-quarter Jewish. Although I will most likely assume a large portion of our child care when we have children, my wife and I will probably use some form of outside child care. Most likely, we would not employ a Black nanny, even if we lived in New York City, but I could not help feeling a sense of guilt and shame when I read the article. I could understand Barbra's wish to use acts of kindness to overlook inequalities of class and race; her desire to equate winning the affections of a Black servant with the absolution of historical and collective guilt. I would not, in the end, act like Barbra, but I do recognize her feelings.

At the same time, I also recognize and identify with the anger Bertha feels toward her white employer. In part, Bertha's anger is a recognition of how profoundly race has affected her and Barbra's lives, and also that Barbra does not truly understand this fact. Although generalizations like this can sometimes be misused – more about this later – American culture defines white middle-class culture as the norm. As a result, Blacks and other colored minorities, must generally know two cultures to survive – the culture of middle-class whites and their own minority culture. Middle-class whites need only to know one culture. For them, knowledge of a minority culture is a seeming – and I use the word "seeming" here purposely – luxury; they can survive without it.

On a smaller scale than Bertha I have experienced the inability of members of the white majority to understand how race has affected my life, to come to terms with the differences between us. Sometimes I can bridge this gap, but never completely; more often, a gulf appears between me and white friends that has previously been unacknowledged. I point out to them that the images I grew up with in the media were all white, that the books I read in school – from Dick and Jane onwards – were about whites and later, about European civilization. I point out to them the way beauty is defined in our culture and how, under such definitions, slanted eyes, flat noses, and round faces just don't make it. And as I talk, I often sense their confusion, the limits of their understanding of the world. They become angry, defensive. "We all have experiences others can't relate to," they reply and equate the issue of race with prejudice against women or Italians or rich people. Such generalizations can sometimes be used to express sympathy with victims of prejudice, but as used by many whites, it generally attempts to shut down racial anger by denying the distinct causes of that anger, thereby rendering it meaningless. Another form of this tactic is the reply, "I think of you just as a white person," or, a bit less chauvinistically, "I think of you as an individual." While, at one time in my life, I would have taken this for a compliment, my reply now is, "I don't want to be a white person. Why can't I be who I am? Why can't you think of me as a Japanese-American *and* as an individual?"

I'd like to leave these questions a moment and, because I'm a writer, take up these themes in terms of literature. In my talks with whites about race, I very quickly find myself referring to history. As many have pointed out, America has never come to terms with two fundamental historical events: the enslavement of Blacks by whites and the taking of this continent by Europeans from the Native Americans and the accompanying policies of genocide. A third historical event that America hasn't come to terms with – and yet is closer to doing so than with the other two – is the internment of Japanese-Americans during World War II. Although some maintain that the camps were caused simply by wartime hysteria, the determining factors were racism and a desire for the property owned by the Japanese-Americans. Recently, in *War Without Mercy,* John Dower has demonstrated how the war in the Pacific, on both sides, took on racist overtones and used racist propaganda that were absent in the war in Europe. In wartime propaganda, while the Nazis were somehow kept separate from the rest of the German race, the Japanese, as a race, were characterized as lice and vermin. This racist propaganda was both caused by and intensified a phenomenon that led to the internment camps: A large number of white Americans were unable to distinguish between the Japanese as the enemy and Japanese-Americans.

Knowing the history behind the camps, knowing that during the internment the lives of many Japanese-Americans, particularly the Issei (first generation), were permanently disrupted; knowing the internment caused the loss of millions of dollars of property, I, as a Japanese-American, feel a kinship to both Blacks and Native Americans that I do not feel with white Americans. It is a kinship that comes from our histories as victims of injustice. Of course, our histories are more than simply being victims, and we must recognize that these histories are also separate and distinct, but there is a certain power and solace in this kinship.

This kinship is reinforced by our current position as minorities in a white-dominated culture. For instance, when Blacks or Native Americans or Chicanos complain about their image in the media, it is a complaint I easily understand. I myself have written a number of pieces about this subject, analyses of the stereotypes in such films as *Rambo* or *Year of the Dragon*. Recently, I read a play by a Sansei playwright, Philip Kan Gotanda, *Yankee Dawg You Die*, and I was struck by the similarities between this play about two Japanese-American actors and Robert Townsend's *Hollywood Shuffle*, a film about a Black actor trying to make it in Hollywood.

In both works, the actors must struggle with the battle between economics and integrity, between finding no parts or playing in roles that stereotype their minority. In *Hollywood Shuffle*, we see the hero, clearly a middle-class Black, trying and failing to portray a pimp in his bathroom mirror. Later in the film, there is a mock Black acting school where Black actors learn to talk in jive, to move like a pimp, to play runaway slaves, to shuffle their feet. In *Yankee Dawg You Die*, a young third-generation Japanese-American actor, Bradley, is fired at one point because he will not mix up his r's and l's when playing a waiter. Throughout the play, he keeps chastizing an older Japanese-American actor for selling out, for playing stereotyped "coolie" and "dirty Jap" parts. Essentially, what Bradley is accusing Vincent of being is a Tom:

> The Business. You keep talking about the business. The industry. Hollywood. What's Hollywood? Cutting up your face to look more white? So my nose is a little flat. Fine! Flat is beautiful. So I don't have a double fold in my eye-lid. Great! No one in my entire racial family has had it in the last 10,000 years.
>
> My old girlfriend used to put scotch tape on her eyelids to get the double folds so she could look more "cau-ca-sian." My

new girlfriend – she doesn't mess around, she got surgery. Where does it stop? "I never turned down a role." Where does it begin? Vincent? Where does it begin? All that self hate. You and your Charlie Chop Suey roles.

Vincent tells Bradley that he knows nothing about the difficulties he, Vincent, went through: "You want to know the truth? I'm glad I did it . . . in some small way it is a victory. Yes, a victory. At least an oriental was on the screen acting, being seen. We existed!" At this point, the scene slides into a father and son mode, where the father-figure, Vincent, tells Bradley that he should appreciate what those who went before him have done; it's easy now for Bradley to spout the rhetoric of Asian-American consciousness, but in the past, such rhetoric was unthinkable. (Earlier in the play, when Vincent says, "I do not really notice, or quite frankly care, if someone is oriental or caucasian . . ." Bradley makes a certain connection between Asian-American rights and other liberation movements. "It's Asian, not oriental," he says. "Asian, oriental. Black, negro. Woman, girl. Gay, homosexual.")

But Bradley then gets on a soapbox and makes a cogent point, though a bit baldly, and I can easily imagine a young Black actor making a similar argument to an old Black actor who has done Stepin Fetchit roles:

> You seem to think that every time you do one of those demeaning roles, all that is lost is your dignity . . . Don't you realize that every time you do a portrayal like that millions of people in their homes, in movie theatres across the country will see it. Be influenced by it. Believe it. Every time you do any old stereotypic role just to pay the bills, you kill the right of some Asian-American child to be treated as a human being. To walk through the school yard and not be called a "chinaman gook" by some taunting kids who just saw the last Rambo film.

By the end of the play, though, it's clear Bradley's been beaten down. After scrambling through failed audition after audition, wanting to make it in the business, he cries when he fails to get a role as a butler because he doesn't know kung fu. He also reveals he has recently had his nose fixed, á la Michael Jackson.

What do the similarities I've been pointing out mean for an Asian-American writer? Recently, there have been a spate of books, such as Allan Bloom's *The Closing of the American Mind*, which call for a return to the classics and a notion of a core-cultural tradition; these critiques bemoan the relativism and "nihilism" of the sixties and the multicultural movements which, in the name of "tolerance," have supposedly left our culture in a shambles. Unfortunately, such critics never really question the political and historical bases of cultural response. If they did, they would understand why, contrary to Allan Bloom, other minority writers represent a valuable resource for Asian-American writers and vice versa: our themes and difficulties are similar; we learn from each other things we cannot receive from a Saul Bellow or John Updike or even Rousseau or Plato.

It is not just the work of Asian-American writers like Gotanda that sustain me. I know a key point in my life was when I discovered the work of Frantz Fanon, particularly his book, *Black Skin, White Masks*. My experience with that work and others like it shows why multiculturalism, for a member of a racial minority, is not simply tolerance, but an essential key to survival.

In his work, Fanon, a Black psychologist, provides a cogent analysis of how a majority can oppress a minority through culture: it makes the victim or servant identify with the ruler and, in so doing, causes the victim to direct whatever anger he/she feels at the situation towards himself/herself in the form of self-hatred.

> In the Antilles ... in the magazines, the Wolf, the Devil, the Evil Spirit, the Bad Man, the Savage are always symbolized by Negroes or Indians; since there is always identification with the victor, the little Negro, quite as easily as the little white boy, becomes an explorer, an adventurer, a missionary "who faces

the danger of being eaten by the wicked Negroes"... The black school boy... who in his lessons is forever talking about "our ancestors, the Gauls," identifies himself with the explorer, the bringer of civilization, the white man who carries truth to the savages – an all-white truth... the young Negro... invests the hero, who is white, with all his own aggression – at that age closely linked to sacrificial dedication, a sacrificial dedication permeated with sadism.

This passage can be taken as another version of Bradley's speech to Vincent on the effects of stereotypes on an Asian-American child.

Fanon was incredibly aware of how the economic, social, and political relations of power create and warp an individual's psychic identity. He was quick to point out that psychic sickness does not always find its source in the neuroses of an individual or that individual's family, but in the greater sickness of a society. In such cases, for the individual to become healthy, he or she must recognize that society is sick, and that the ideas he or she has received from that society are part of that sickness.

In short, what Fanon recognized and taught me was the liberating power of anger.

After reading Fanon and the Black French poet from Martinique, Aime Cesaire, I wrote a number of poems in which I chose to ally myself with people of color, anti-colonialist movements, and a non-Eurocentric consciousness. When writing these poems, I was aware of how such poems can often become vehicles for slogans and cheap rhetoric; still I tried to discover a language with a denseness which would prevent such reduction, increase thought, and turn words like "gook" and "nigger" against their original meaning, bending and realigning the slang of racism. Here is the ending of one of those poems:

> ... and we were all good niggers, good gooks and japs, good spics and rice eaters saying mem sab, sahib, bwana, boss-san, señor, father, heartthrob oh honored and most unceasing, oh

devisor and provider of our own obsequious, ubiquitous ugliness, which stares at you baboon-like, banana-like, dwarf-like, tortoise-like, dirt-like, slant-eyed, kink-haired, ashen and pansied and brutally unredeemable, we are whirling about you, tartars of the air all the urinating, tarantula grasping, ant multiplying, succubused, hothouse hoards yes, it us, it us, we, we knockee, yes, sir, massa, boss-san, we tearee down your door!

I was scared at first by the anger of this poem, but I also saw it as an answer, an antidote to the depression I had been feeling, a depression brought on by a lack of self-worth and by my dropping out of English graduate school. As my therapist had told me, depression is the repression of anger and grief. In my diary I wrote about the unlocking of this repression:

> In the first stages of such a process, one can enter a position where the destruction of one stereotype creates merely a new stereotype, and where the need to point out injustice overwhelms and leaves the writing with a baldness that seems both naive and sentimental. Still, the task must be faced, and what I am now trying to do in both my writing and my life is to replace self-hatred and self-negation with anger and grief over my lost selves, over the ways my cultural heritage has been denied to me, over the ways that people in America would assume either that I am not American or, conversely, that I am just like them; over the ways my education and the values of European culture have denied that other cultures exist. I know more about Europe at the time when my grandfather came to America than I know about Meiji Japan. I know Shakespeare and Donne, Sophocles and Homer better than I know Zeami, Bashō or Lady Murasaki. This is not to say I regret what I know, but I do regret what I don't know. And the argument that the culture of America is derived from Europe will not wipe away this regret.

I am convinced if I had not read Fanon, if I had not reached these insights, and gone on to explore beyond white European culture, I would have died as a writer and died spiritually and psychically as a person. I would have ended up

denying who I am and my place in history. Thus, I think that
to deny a people a right to determine their own cultural tradition is a type of genocide.

Of course, arguing for multiculturalism is not the same thing
as saying that, as a minority writer, I don't need to read the
works of European culture. It's not a case of either/or. As
Carlos Fuentes remarked, "We [Latin Americans] have to
know the cultures of the West even better than a Frenchman
or an Englishman, and at the same time we have to know our
own cultures. This sometimes means going back to the Indian
cultures, whereas the Europeans feel they don't have to know
our cultures at all. We have to know Quetzalcoatl and Descartes. They think Descartes is enough." I think Fuentes
would agree with Jesse Jackson that there was something
wrong with those students who greeted his appearance at
Stanford with the chant, "Hey hey, ho ho/Western culture's
got to go." As Jackson pointed out, Western culture was their
culture. It is difficult to strike an appropriate balance.

In the same issue of the *Village Voice* that the article about
the Black nannies appeared, Stanley Crouch wrote a percep-
tive, challenging critique of James Baldwin. Crouch argues
that at the beginning of Baldwin's career, Baldwin was able to
maneuver his way through subtleties of the Black writer's
position. As an example of this, Crouch cites Baldwin's dis-
tinction between sociology and literature in evaluating the
work of Richard Wright; Baldwin argues that despite the
good intentions of protest novels, they cannot succeed if they
are "badly written and wildly improbable." Still Crouch main-
tains that very early Baldwin's vision began to blur, and cites
this passage from the essay, "Stranger in the Village," a depiction of Baldwin's visit to a Swiss town and his sense of alienation from its people:

> These people cannot be, from the point of view of power,
> strangers anywhere in the world; they have made the modern
> world, in effect, even if they do not know it. The most illiterate

among them is related, in a way that I am not, to Dante, Shakespeare, Michaelangelo, Aeschylus, da Vinci, Rembrandt, and
Racine; the cathedral at Chartres says something to them that it
cannot say to me, as indeed would New York's Empire State
Building, should anyone here ever see it. Out of their hymns
and dances come Beethoven and Bach. Go back a few centuries
and they are in their full glory – but I am in Africa, watching
the conquerors arrive.

Crouch charges Baldwin with slipping into a simplistic dualis-
tic thinking, with letting his rage create a we–they attitude
which denies the complexity of the race situation:

Such thinking lead to the problems we still face in which too
many so-called nonwhite people look upon "the West" as some
catchall in which every European or person of European descent is somehow part of a structure bent solely on excluding or
intimidating the Baldwins of the world. Were Roland Hayes,
Marian Anderson, Leontyne Price, Jessye Norman, or Kiri Te
Kanawa to have taken such a position, they would have locked
themselves out of a world of music that originated neither
among Afro-Americans nor Maoris. Further, his ahistorical ignorance is remarkable, and perhaps willful.

If Baldwin's position is that Afro-Americans cannot learn,
or enjoy or perform European culture, or that European culture is worthless to an Afro-American, that is nonsense. But
that is not Baldwin's position. He is simply arguing that his
relationship to that culture is different from a white European; he views that culture through the experience of a Black
American, and if he is to be faulted, it is because he does not
give a detailed enough explanation of how his experience as a
Black American informs his experience of European culture.
But none of this – including the success of opera stars like
Jessye Norman – negates the fact that, in America and Europe, European culture has political – that is, ideological –
effects and one effect is to reinforce the political power of
those of European descent and to promote a view of whites as

superior to coloreds. (It is not the only effect of that culture, but again, neither Baldwin nor I am arguing that it is.)

Crouch goes on to argue that "breaking through the mask of collective whiteness – collective guilt – that Baldwin imposes would demand recognition of the fact that, as history and national chauvinism prove, Europe is not a one-celled organism." I will say more about collective guilt a bit later, but it is interesting to note that Crouch refuses the concept of collectivity when it comes to guilt, yet at the same time charges that Baldwin refuses to entertain the possibility of "the international wonder of human heritage." Guilt can never be held collectively, but culture, specifically European culture, can be universal.

Yet, at the same time Crouch argues the non-exclusivity of European culture, he chastizes Baldwin for taking the themes of Third-World writers and adapting them to the context of America: "the denial by Europeans of non-Western cultural complexity – or parity; the social function of the inferiority complex colonialism threw over the native like a net; the alignment of Christianity and cruelty under colonialism, and the idea that world views were at odds, European versus the 'spirit of Bandung,' or the West in the ring with the Third World." How sharp the boundaries of culture should be is a difficult question; it may seem that both Crouch and Baldwin want things both ways: they just disagree on which cultures can attain universality, European culture or that of the Third World. To sort out the specifics of each of their cases requires us to connect attitudes towards culture with feelings about race, specifically the rage of Blacks and other colored minorities in America.

As I've already argued with my own reading of Frantz Fanon, I do think it is illuminating and useful to use Third-World problems in looking at the race issue in America. Still, I also agree with Crouch that there are fundamental differences between the position of Blacks in America and that of colonials in the Third World. To forget these differences in a desire to be at one with all oppressed peoples is both false and dangerous. And I recognize that when borrowing or learning from the language of Third-World peoples and American Blacks, Japanese-Americans, like myself, must still recognize fundamental differences between our position and that of other people of color, whether here or in the Third World.

Part of the danger is that if we ignore the specifics of the situation of our own minority group, in essence we both deny who we are and our own complexity. We also run the risk of using our victimhood as a mask for sainthood, of letting whatever sins the white race has committed against us become a permanent absolution for us, an excuse to forgo moral and psychological introspection. Crouch argues somewhat convincingly that this is exactly the trap that Baldwin fell into and cites as evidence Baldwin's remark that "Rage can only with difficulty, and never entirely, be brought under the domination of the intelligence and is therefore not susceptible to any arguments whatever." According to Crouch, Baldwin, as his career progressed, sold out to rage, despair, self-righteousness, and a will to scandalize:

> In America . . . fat-mouthing Negroes . . . chose to sneer at the heroic optimism of the Civil Rights Movement; they developed their own radical chic and spoke of Malcom X as being beyond compromise, of his unwillingness to cooperate with the white man, and of his ideas of being too radical for assimilation. Baldwin was sucked into this world of intellectual airlessness. By *The Fire Next Time,* Baldwin is so happy to see white policemen made uncomfortable by Muslim rallies, and so willing to embrace almost anything that disturbs whites in general, that he starts competing with the apocalyptic tone of the Nation of Islam.

In focusing on Baldwin's inability to transform or let go his rage, I feel Crouch finally hits upon something. I also feel a shudder of self-recognition. Yet the condition Crouch pictures here is a bit more complex than he admits. Certainly, a convincing argument can be made that King's appeal to a higher yet common morality was and will be more effective than Malcom X's in changing the hearts and minds of whites in America, yet in his very approach to the problem, Crouch seems to put the burden for change upon the Black minority rather than on the white majority. There is something intellectually and morally dishonest about this. For whether one judges King's philosophy or Malcom X's as correct depends in part on a reading of the hearts and minds of white Americans. If those hearts and minds are fiercely unchanging, then Malcom X's might seem the more logical stance. Either way, it is a judgment call and it involves a great deal of uncertainty, especially since that judgment involves actions in the future. Yet nowhere in his argument does Crouch concede this.

Shaw called hatred the coward's revenge for ever having been intimidated, says Crouch, and Crouch sees this hatred as the basis of Baldwin's attitude towards whites and towards European culture. I find something skewed in Crouch's use of Shaw's quip here. Given the history of race in America, equating a Black man's sense of intimidation solely with cowardice seems a simplification; couldn't that intimidation in many cases be an acknowledgment of reality? Admittedly, there is in Baldwin that self-righteousness, that rage not quite under control. I know myself how easy it is to give in to it. But Crouch's approach to the dialectics of rage seems to me entirely unrealistic. In my poem, "Song For Artaud, Fanon, Cesaire, Uncle Tom, Tonto and Mr. Moto," I recognize a certain demagogic tone, a triumphant and self-righteous bitterness and rage. And yet, I also recognize that my rage needed to be released, that it had been held back in my own psyche for too many years, held back within my family, and held back within my race in America. That rage was liberating for me, just as it is for any oppressed people. As should be obvious to anyone, those who are oppressed cannot change their situation, cannot own themselves, unless they finally own their rage at their condition and those who have caused it. Crouch seems to have wanted Baldwin to overcome or stand above this rage, but there is a certain wishful thinking in this. One does not overcome or stand above this rage: one first goes through it, and then leaves it behind.

The problem is that this process is both long and complicated and neither Crouch nor Baldwin quite understands what it entails: one must learn first how liberating anger feels, then how intoxicating, then how damaging, and in each of these stages, the reason for these feelings must be admitted and accurately described. It may be argued that Baldwin accomplished the first of these tasks – the liberation that comes from rage – and that he alluded or hinted at the second – the intoxication that comes from rage – and even at times alluded or hinted at the third, but for the most, because he never accurately described how intoxicating the rage he felt was, he could never see how damaging it was.

For it is intoxicating after years of feeling inferior, after years of hating oneself, it is so comforting to use this rage not just to feel equal to the oppressor, but superior, and not just superior, but simply blameless and blessed, one of the prophetic and holy ones. It is what one imagines a god feels like, and in this state one does feel like a god of history, a fate; one knows that history is on one's side, because one is helping to break open, to recreate history. And how much better it is to feel like a god after years of worshipping the oppressor as one.

But once one can clearly describe all this, one realizes that such a stance represents a new form of hubris, an intoxicating blindness: human beings are not gods, are not superior to other human beings. Human beings are fallible, cannot foresee the future, cannot demand or receive freely the worship of others. In aligning one's rage with a sense of superiority, one fails to recognize how this rage is actually fueled by a sense of inferiority: one's own version of history and views on equality need, on some level, the approval, the assent, the defeat of the oppressor. The wish for superiority is simply the reverse side of feeling inferior, not its cure. It focuses all the victim's problems on the other, the oppressor. Yet until it is recognized how one has contributed to this victimhood, the chains are still there, inside, are part of the psyche. Conversely, liberation occurs only when one is sure enough of oneself, feels good enough, to admit fault, admit their portion of blame.

Given the difficulty of this process, it's no wonder so many stumble in the process or stop midway through. And it is made much more difficult if the oppressor is especially recalcitrant, is implacable towards change. When this happens, fresh wound after fresh wound is inflicted, causing bundle after bundle of rage: bitterness then becomes too tempting; too much energy is required to heal. To his credit, Crouch shows some understanding of this fact in relationship to Baldwin: "Perhaps it is understandable that Baldwin could not resist the contemptuous pose of militance that gave focus to all of his anger for being the homely duckling, who never became a swan, the writer who would perhaps never have been read by so many Black people otherwise, and the homosexual who lived abroad most of his adult life in order to enjoy his preferences."

In the end, though, Crouch never comes to terms with the sources of Baldwin's rage. One reason for this is Crouch's belief that "collective whiteness – and *collective guilt*" were merely a mask, a simplification for Baldwin.

Part of Crouch's problem is that he distorts Baldwin's position. On the one hand, it is a simplification to pretend that collective whiteness and collective guilt are the *only* ways to view the race situation in America. But it is not a simplification to say that collective whiteness and collective white guilt *do exist*. The superior economic and political power of whites as compared to colored minorities in this country is a fact, and on some level, every white in this country benefits from that power. Of course, this does not mean that every white has more economic and political power than every member of the colored minorities. But it is not just this inequality of power that makes collective white guilt a fact; it is the way that power was acquired and the way its sources have been kept hidden from the consciousness of both whites and colored minorities that makes this term applicable.

Here I return to the fundamental historical events I mentioned earlier in this essay: the enslavement of Blacks, the taking of Native American land and the genocidal policies that accomplished it. One can think of other related historical events: the internment camps, the Asian-Exclusion act, the conditions of the Asian workers building the American railroads, the conditions of migrant farm workers and illegal aliens. The list could go on and on. But that is to point out the obvious. What is not so obvious is how the laws of property in our society have served to make permanent what was stolen in the past. Those who bought my grandparents' property for a song still benefit from that property today; there has been no compensation, just as there has been no compensation to Blacks for the institution of slavery or to Native Americans for the taking of a continent and the destruction of their peoples and culture. And as long as there is no movement toward a just compensation, the collective guilt will remain.

And yet I also recognize that a just compensation is not possible. The wrongs are too great, run too far back in history, and human beings are fallible and forgetful. Justice demands too high a price.

Therefore we must settle for less, for a compromise. The concept of white collective guilt reminds us of this compromise, that there has been and probably will always be a less than even settling of the debt. However whites protest that they want equality and justice, they are, in the end, not willing to pay the price. And when those they have wronged call for the price, the reaction of whites is almost always one of anger and resentment.

Now, in this situation, the whites have two choices. When they accept the concept of collective guilt, they admit that they feel unjustifiable anger and resentment at any measure that threatens any part of their privileged position, much less any of the measures that approach just compensation. When whites don't admit collective guilt, they try to blame racial troubles on those who ask for a just settlement and remain baffled at the anger and resentment of the colored minorities.

Whether in the area of culture or in economic relations, these choices remain. In the realm of culture in America, white European culture has held the floor for centuries; just as with any one-sided conversation, a balance can only be achieved if the speaker who has dominated speaks less and listens more. That is what conservative cultural critics are unwilling to do; for them there is no such thing as collective guilt, much less the obligation such guilt bestows. It is not just that the colored minorities in America need to create and receive their own cultural images, nor that, for these minorities, the culture of the Third World and its struggles against white-dominated cultures provides insights into race in America that cannot be found in European literature. This much ought to seem obvious. But there is more: only when whites in America begin to listen to the voices of the colored minorities and the Third World will they come to understand not just those voices but also themselves and their world. Reality is not simply knowing who we think we are, but also what others think of us. And only with this knowledge will whites ever understand what needs to be done to make things equal.

The situation in the *Voice* article on nannies is no different: without admitting the concept of collective guilt, the white middle-class Barbra remains unable to comprehend her nanny Bertha, unable to understand what this Black woman feels. Ultimately, Barbra does not want to admit that the only way she is going to feel comfortable with Bertha is if they meet as equals; that society must be changed so that Barbra and her children will not enjoy certain privileges they have taken as rights. In short, Barbra and other whites will have to give up power; that is what it means to make things equal. At the same time she must admit that no matter how much she

works for change, how much society changes, there will
never, on this earth, be a just settling of accounts. That is the
burden she has to take up; she may think it will destroy her,
but it will not. And, ultimately, this process would not only
help Bertha to meet and know Barbra as an equal, but for
Barbra to understand and accept who she is, to know herself.

ISHMAEL REED

America:

The Multinational Society

At the annual Lower East Side Jewish Festival yesterday, a
Chinese woman ate a pizza slice in front of Ty Thuan Duc's
Vietnamese grocery store. Beside her a Spanish-speaking family patronized a cart with two signs: "Italian Ices" and "Kosher
by Rabbi Alper." And after the pastrami ran out, everybody ate
knishes.

(New York Times, 23 June 1983)

On the day before Memorial Day, 1983, a poet called me to
describe a city he had just visited. He said that one section
included mosques, built by the Islamic people who dwelled
there. Attending his reading, he said, were large numbers of
Hispanic people, forty thousand of whom lived in the same
city. He was not talking about a fabled city located in some
mysterious region of the world. The city he'd visited was
Detroit.

A few months before, as I was leaving Houston, Texas, I
heard it announced on the radio that Texas's largest minority
was Mexican-American, and though a foundation recently
issued a report critical of bilingual education, the taped voice
used to guide the passengers on the air trams connecting
terminals in Dallas Airport is in both Spanish and English. If

the trend continues, a day will come when it will be difficult to travel through some sections of the country without hearing commands in both English and Spanish; after all, for some western states, Spanish was the first written language and the Spanish style lives on in the western way of life.

Shortly after my Texas trip, I sat in an auditorium located on the campus of the University of Wisconsin at Milwaukee as a Yale professor – whose original work on the influence of African cultures upon those of the Americas has led to his ostracism from some monocultural intellectual circles – walked up and down the aisle, like an old-time southern evangelist, dancing and drumming the top of the lectern, illustrating his points before some serious Afro-American intellectuals and artists who cheered and applauded his performance and his mastery of information. The professor was "white." After his lecture, he joined a group of Milwaukeeans in a conversation. All of the participants spoke Yoruban, though only the professor had ever traveled to Africa.

One of the artists told me that his paintings, which included African and Afro-American mythological symbols and imagery, were hanging in the local McDonald's restaurant. The next day I went to McDonald's and snapped pictures of smiling youngsters eating hamburgers below paintings that could grace the walls of any of the country's leading museums. The manager of the local McDonald's said, "I don't know what you boys are doing, but I like it," as he commissioned the local painters to exhibit in his restaurant.

Such blurring of cultural styles occurs in everyday life in the United States to a greater extent than anyone can imagine and is probably more prevalent than the sensational conflict between people of different backgrounds that is played up and often encouraged by the media. The result is what the Yale professor, Robert Thompson, referred to as a cultural bouillabaisse, yet members of the nation's present educational and cultural Elect still cling to the notion that the United States belongs to some vaguely defined entity they refer to as "Western civilization," by which they mean, presumably, a civilization created by the people of Europe, as if Europe can be viewed in monolithic terms. Is Beethoven's Ninth Symphony, which includes Turkish marches, a part of Western civilization, or the late nineteenth- and twentieth-century French paintings, whose creators were influenced by Japanese art? And what of the cubists, through whom the influence of African art changed modern painting, or the surrealists, who were so impressed with the art of the Pacific Northwest Indians that, in their map of North America, Alaska dwarfs the lower forty-eight in size?

Are the Russians, who are often criticized for their adoption of "Western" ways by Tsarist dissidents in exile, members of Western civilization? And what of the millions of Europeans who have black African and Asian ancestry, black Africans having occupied several countries for hundreds of years? Are these "Europeans" members of Western civilization, or the Hungarians, who originated across the Urals in a place called Greater Hungary, or the Irish, who came from the Iberian Peninsula?

Even the notion that North America is part of Western civilization because our "system of government" is derived from Europe is being challenged by Native American historians who say that the founding fathers, Benjamin Franklin especially, were actually influenced by the system of government that had been adopted by the Iroquois hundreds of years prior to the arrival of large numbers of Europeans.

Western civilization, then, becomes another confusing category like Third World, or Judeo-Christian culture, as man attempts to impose his small-screen view of political and cultural reality upon a complex world. Our most publicized novelist recently said that Western civilization was the greatest achievement of mankind, an attitude that flourishes on the street level as scribbles in public restrooms: "White Power," "Niggers and Spics Suck," or "Hitler was a prophet," the latter being the most telling, for wasn't Adolph Hitler the archetypal monoculturalist who, in his pigheaded arrogance, believed that one way and one blood was so pure that it had to be protected from alien strains at all costs? Where did such an attitude, which has caused so much misery and depression in our national life, which has tainted even our noblest achievements, begin? An attitude that caused the incarceration of Japanese-American citizens during World War II, the persecution of Chicanos and Chinese-Americans, the near-extermination of the Indians, and the murder and lynchings of thousands of Afro-Americans.

Virtuous, hardworking, pious, even though they occasionally would wander off after some fancy clothes, or rendezvous in the woods with the town prostitute, the Puritans are idealized in our schoolbooks as "a hardy band" of no-nonsense patriarchs whose discipline razed the forest and brought order to the New World (a term that annoys Native American historians). Industrious, responsible, it was their "Yankee ingenuity" and practicality that created the work ethic. They were simple folk who produced a number of good poets, and they set the tone for the American writing style, of lean and spare lines, long before Hemingway. They worshiped in churches whose colors blended in with the New England snow, churches with simple structures and ornate lecterns.

The Puritans were a daring lot, but they had a mean streak. They hated the theater and banned Christmas. They punished people in a cruel and inhuman manner. They killed children who disobeyed their parents. When they came in contact with those whom they considered heathens or aliens, they behaved in such a bizarre and irrational manner that this chapter in the American history comes down to us as a late-movie horror film. They exterminated the Indians, who taught them how to survive in a world unknown to them, and their encounter with the calypso culture of Barbados resulted in what the tourist guide in Salem's Witches' House refers to as the Witchcraft Hysteria.

The Puritan legacy of hard work and meticulous accounting led to the establishment of a great industrial society; it is no wonder that the American industrial revolution began in Lowell, Massachusetts, but there was the other side, the strange and paranoid attitudes toward those different from the Elect.

The cultural attitudes of that early Elect continue to be voiced in everyday life in the United States: the president of a distinguished university, writing a letter to the *Times,* belittling the study of African civilizations; the television network that promoted its show on the Vatican art with the boast that this art represented "the finest achievements of the human spirit." A modern up-tempo state of complex rhythms that depends upon contacts with an international community can no longer behave as if it dwelled in a "Zion Wilderness" surrounded by beasts and pagans.

When I heard a schoolteacher warn the other night about the invasion of the American educational system by foreign curriculums, I wanted to yell at the television set, "Lady, they're already here." It has already begun because the world is here. The world has been arriving at these shores for at least ten thousand years from Europe, Africa, and Asia. In the late nineteenth and early twentieth centuries, large numbers of Europeans arrived, adding their cultures to those of the European, African, and Asian settlers who were already here, and recently millions have been entering the country from South America and the Caribbean, making Yale Professor Bob Thompson's bouillabaisse richer and thicker.

One of our most visionary politicians said that he envisioned a time when the United States could become the brain of the world, by which he meant the repository of all of the latest advanced information systems. I thought of that remark when an enterprising poet friend of mine called to say that he had just sold a poem to a computer magazine and that the editors were delighted to get it because they didn't carry fiction or poetry. Is that the kind of world we desire? A humdrum homogeneous world of all brains and no heart, no fiction, no poetry; a world of robots with human attendants bereft of imagination, of culture? Or does North America deserve a more exciting destiny? To become a place where the cultures of the world crisscross. This is possible because the United States is unique in the world: The world is here.

MICHELE WALLACE

Invisibility Blues

Once again, the talking heads at "MacNeil-Lehrer" have re-
wound and are playing for the umpteenth go-round their
so-called discussion of Jesse Jackson, the-cause-not-the-
campaign, the-man-who-can't-win, the mystery meat in the
party's platform who will blow-the-chance-of-a-Democratic-
victory-in-November. Needless to say, they pointedly neglect
to make reference to a Rainbow Coalition. It often seems to
me that the so-called media pundits must sleep in coffins at
night, and never venture beyond Greenwich, Connecticut
during the day. Where else could they be getting their
information?

Consider the *Sunday New York Times* "Week in Review" on
Jackson's triumph in Michigan: "Still, let it be recorded that
for at least one week in American history, in a middle-sized
Midwestern state, a broad range of white voters took the
presidential candidacy of a black man with utmost serious-
ness." "Let it be recorded" by whom? How did it get to be
"American history" when it just happened? Why is it only the
disposition of "white voters" that "American history" needs
to record? Is the use of the verb "to take" to be understood as
a Freudian slip of the political unconscious?

Perhaps most objectionable is the underlying assumption
of white-bread discourse, which is that while the writer is

162 THE GRAYWOLF ANNUAL

perfectly willing to consider the Jackson candidacy – despite the fact that Jackson is black – the most racist voters in the party are not. Therefore, the proposition must be shelved indefinitely because, as everybody knows, racism expresses the will of the party, the will of the people, and the only show in town. Which is exactly the attitude I expected a nearly lily-white mass media to take. In 1985, blacks held 3.5 percent of newsroom jobs, "hispanics" 1.7 percent, and the notorious "other" (whom postmodernists claim encompasses everybody but them) a whopping 1.1 percent according to The American Society of Newspapers. These figures appeared in *Newsweek* in late 1986 in an article emphasizing the lack of minorities – blacks really – in management positions in the media. The article was called "No Room at the Top." But the story between the lines was that the media was the U.S. private industry with the least progressive affirmative action profile. "Nearly 60 percent of daily newspapers employ no minorities at all," *Newsweek* said then. "Magazines are even worse; TV and radio only slightly better." And I don't imagine the situation has improved.

As Jackson's comet refused to die a "natural" death, the media kindly manufactured a climax for him – the way you compose a suspense novel – and then the antagonist *has* to die because the plot dictates it. But it's not over yet. In the words of the anonymous black pundits of my youth, it ain't over till it's over. Or as James Baldwin put it in *Notes of a Native Son,* "This world is white no longer, and it will never be white again."

Crossing the Finish Line

Every time the media starts their woefully inadequate coverage of the Jackson campaign – the dichotomizing of Jews and blacks in New York was particularly painful – I am reminded of the day the Kenyan ran in and won the New York Marathon. I am no sports follower, and Gene, my spouse equivalent and I, were about to run ourselves, but because the

19-inch screen Mitsubishi color TV is the central thing in our tiny New York apartment – kind of like an altar – we had a habit of turning it on to verify that there was nothing worth watching before we made any major moves. Usually on Sunday morning – well, we know what's on Sunday morning – but what we saw and heard that Sunday morning was spellbinding, like watching a real life illustration of invisibility. For the last several miles of the race, the Kenyan was in the lead by half a mile. Or so it seemed on the screen via one camera which showed the Kenyan running alone and via another camera, some place else entirely, which showed a gaggle of white male runners-up.

Yet a flock of white male commentators endlessly speculated on the probability of his losing. They considered it from every angle and still it made no sense. Did they imagine he would drop dead from blackness? Just as he was about to cross the finish line – and these white male reporters were forced to acknowledge that clearly he would be the winner – the camera left him. We never saw him cross the finish line although our eyes were riveted to the screen waiting for them to come back to it. Okay, we told each other, they made a mistake. They're upset because a black man has won the New York Marathon for the first time. But we were not down in Plains, Georgia somewhere talking to members of Jimmy Carter's church. They'll catch themselves soon enough. They'll show a playback or slow motion or something. We watched in disbelief as the white men narrated the second- and third-place finish of white male runners, then the much later finish of the white female winner. Does that mean that winning is all in the eyes of the beholder or the cameras? I don't know.

I only know that MacNeil-Lehrer and even Charlayne Hunter-Gault are disappointing. Yes, even Hunter-Gault, even though she's the black woman who once integrated the University of Georgia in the Civil Rights Movement. For years I've been holding on to the fantasy that Gault was being snide and cynical beneath her modified Southern accent. Such as when she questioned white male economists closely during Wall Street's so-called "Black Monday" about where was their "trickle-down" now? Of course, that "Black Monday" business made me and every other black American wonder whether it was 1887 or 1987. But did Gault say something about how blacks are tired of derogatory references to the color black?

Taking any pride at all in black tokens is much like waiting for Tonto to walk away from the Lone Ranger, or wondering when Rochester will quit Jack Benny's employ, which is how a whole lot of us who aren't white managed to enjoy these programs in the 1950s and 1960s. But this isn't the 1950s. What is a black viewer supposed to wish for Oprah Winfrey, Bill Cosby, Eddie Murphy, Action Jackson, Spike Lee, and Prince? What's changed? Has Tonto walked away from the Lone Ranger yet? Has Rochester handed Benny his notice? And what, if anything, has this tokenism on a grand scale to do with who makes information?

Any black writer less fashionable than Alice Walker or Toni Morrison would be unlikely to be asked to cover the Jackson campaign for a major magazine like *Playboy* or *Vanity Fair.* And even if Morrison or Walker were willing to do it, they would probably catch unmitigated hell about syntax, ideology, and "black pride." What's more, there really is a "trickle down" on small and progressive publishing and press. Once upon a time, people like James Baldwin, John A. Williams, or Gordon Parks were asked to write stories for big magazines, but racism appears to be this continually escalating ideological economy with a mind of its own.

It shouldn't be necessary to remind anybody that during slavery blacks were forbidden by law from reading and writing. Simultaneously, the philosophical wisdom of Western civilization, Henry Louis Gates tells us in his introduction to *"Race," Writing, and Difference,* that the black "race" was constitutionally unable to read and write. We find ourselves in a situation in which, from university to network, it's still assumed that we have no written language.

Thus it really puzzled me when all the white male critics

started bitching about how *Cry Freedom* was a bad movie because it made Stephen Biko's character seem subsidiary to Donald Wood's. It had the impact of trivializing or sentimentalizing Biko's voice, I recall both the *New York Times* and the *Village Voice* saying. Rather I thought that Attenborough – for perverse Anglo reasons of his own, was drawing the obvious connection between conditions for blacks in South Africa (media representation, political underrepresentation, and poverty) and comparable circumstances for blacks in the U.S. Moreover, that Biko's message came to the world via the intervention and interpretation of a white male, that a white male starred in the film version of Biko's story, strikes me as exactly the situation we find ourselves reaping the benefits of in U.S. mass media today. The thing to criticize most about the movie is that it seemed far too much like the United States to ever be South Africa.

No Room at the Inn

Secretary of Education William Bennett, who was quite emphatic in his recent criticism of curricular changes at Stanford University on the "MacNeil-Lehrer NewsHour," charges that "racism" and "sexism" are irrelevant in the context of studying Western civilization. Somehow for him the very words themselves are tainted. Of course, this makes perfect sense to James Lehrer, who interviewed him. In fact, "racism" and "sexism" are irrelevant in every context, as far as they're both concerned.

The first moment at which I really began to understand this attitude was on "Washington Week in Review" when Carl Rowan was given the unpleasant task of trying to explain to a panel of white journalists why Supreme Court Justice Thurgood Marshall had said that Reagan was a racist president. Oh, no, no, no, no, they all insisted. Reagan is not a racist. Not racist, not racist, no, no, they all chanted. Because, after all, nobody is actually racist. Except some anonymous white everyman out in the middle of Michigan, who single-handedly shaped the media's coverage of "the presidential campaign of a black man."

Bennett is not entirely wrong to want to have such words as "racism" and "sexism" dropped from the language. To suggest that not only dead white men have written (and will always write) the crucial text is to threaten the entire notion of knowledge as something timeless, universal, and, therefore, on another plane above the historical and intimate concreteness and specificity of "racism" and "sexism." What Bennett realizes is that there isn't space enough for everybody, not only in the economy but on the book list. Furthermore, if everybody can sit at the table, there won't be any room left at the inn and, pretty soon, people will be doing what? Sleeping on subways and eating out of garbage cans? The distinctions and dichotomies between classics and kitsch, winners and also-rans, are necessary in order to preserve order as we now understand it.

It's not just a matter of white people at the top and people of color at the bottom (although that's often the way it turns out), it's about the notion of order as an arrangement in which some people are always better off than others because it helps foster the inexorable self-loathing that keeps everybody in their place, paying taxes for cops and robbers shenanigans and awaiting the inevitable exposé at the televised hearings.

Catching Up, the Existential Plight

I teach Afro-American literature, feminist literature, and creative writing in the American Studies Department at SUNY–Buffalo. It's a pretty unusual American Studies Department, I suppose, in that it attempts to straddle the dream and the reality of American pluralism. The dream is the Rainbow Coalition in academia, although sometimes it appears that all the contingents would prefer to remain separate. The reality is that minority people – Puerto Rican, Native American, U.S., Afro-American, and Women's Studies Programs, and a

Women of Color component – need to start getting doctorates so that they can head some of the programs, obtain some of the grant money, do some of the research, and write some of the books that shape the academic enterprise and, ultimately, influence the global production of knowledge that keeps us all enthralled.

The department is in the process of defining the requirements for the Ph.D. I'm the token non-Ph.D. involved in all of this. We're trying to make sure that book lists facilitate the integration of programs that will be necessary to students at the Ph.D. level, that the oral and written exams are doable, and that minority students are encouraged, especially in professional competence and intellectual rigor. It is very difficult for me to be involved because every day I understand a little better why I don't have a Ph.D. even though I've tried; why black women, as a rule, don't pursue doctorates; why even when they do, they are often indefinitely delayed.

My Aunt Barbara began her college education in 1942 at Hunter College when she was sixteen (the family pitched in to pay her tuition), completed her bachelor's in nutrition and became a dietician, presumably in 1947, then – while working – did her master in Education at Hunter College at a time when the City University of New York was not keen on admitting black students. I don't know precisely when she completed her master's, although I always thought she spoke the most precise English and read more books than anybody I ever knew. I remember her briefly pursuing her Ph.D. at Columbia, then dropping out because a professor accused her of being illiterate. She was not what most people would consider to be a brave person and she never got over that or a lot of other things. As an elementary school teacher, she grew to hate the public schools. About five years ago she drank herself to death.

Many of the people in my family – starting perhaps with my great-grandfather who was a teacher in Palakta, Florida and the son of ex-slaves – have graduated from college, although somehow it's never brought us much security, or even the certainty that the next generation would be educated. When he died suddenly at an early age, my great-grandfather's oldest children had to come home from school. None of his six children ever finished college. My grandmother dreamed of college for her children instead of for herself. Although my mother and my Aunt Barbara both graduated from college, my uncle never went at all. He became a gang leader called Baron and died of a heroin overdose when I was nine. In my father's family (from Jamaica), the record is just as tattered. Financial ruin, ignorance, and despair seemed to follow us around like badly trained pets wanting food and water.

I was lucky. My grandmother began to teach me how to read before I went to school. My youngest sister, named after Aunt Barbara, would play on the floor around our feet, reciting from memory the words of the stories I was reading. Because I went to private schools and because I was raised in a home where reading and writing were valued above all else, I received a rigorous basic education.

Then I began to attend the City College of New York. In the 1970s, CCNY was undergoing dramatic political upheaval partly due to the open admissions struggle of the late 1960s. The student body was shifting in composition from white to black. Although I was in the English Department, where most black students still feared to tread, the education I received was, nevertheless, shaped by fluctuating standards.

I graduated from CCNY in 1974 with a B.A. in English and Writing without ever having studied any English Literature written prior to 1800. Although I received very classy training in creative writing from the likes of Donald Barthelme and John Hawkes, if it had not been for my private high school education, I would never have read Shakespeare or Chaucer. It was in high school that I encountered Beowulf and the Romantic Poets. As for the Latin and Greek of Virginia Woolf's and W.E.B. Dubois's lamentations, there was never any question. Milton was out.

When I became a book review researcher at *Newsweek* in the fall of 1974, I realized that there were words that were commonly used by writers and fellow researchers that I neither knew how to pronounce nor how to use in a sentence. I began to read a lot, for now I vaguely began to comprehend why my favorite teacher at CCNY had begged me to seek a minority scholarship to Harvard. My reading clarified a lot for me, although not yet the importance of reading itself.

So in the search of validation, I landed in the Ph.D. program in American Studies at Yale and I was lost before I started. I had never heard of Cotton Mather, Jonathan Edwards, Max Weber, Thorstein Veblen, John Dewey, or C. Wright Mills. I had never read John Blassingame, John Hope Franklin, or W.E.B. Dubois. I had read Alice Walker, Kate Millet, James Baldwin, Norman Mailer, and a great many novels, but that seemed to count for nothing. While I could write reasonably well, and I read a lot, the words seemed to escape me when it was time to talk to fellow graduate students. I was morbidly afraid that when I opened my mouth, I would show my bottomless ignorance and make a fool of myself. So I kept to myself and read voraciously but came to loathe the superbly well-educated, articulate whites who shared my classes. I feared I would never catch up. When the fear became too much for me – I was no brave person either – I dropped out. But the project of catching up will always describe my existential plight.

Cultural Detention Centers

Even at SUNY–Buffalo there seems little recognition that increasingly graduate students – especially students of color – need reasons, connections, and explanations if graduate study is to make sense to them. They need to know that people of color have written books, have been intellectually engaged. On the other hand, standards of professional competence, the study of the classics in the field, and intellectual performance should not be dismissed in some misguided liberal attempt to make it easier. Or as Donald Lazere says in *American Media and Mass Culture*, "Pending revolutionary reversal of white and black hegemonic roles in American politics and culture . . . leftists might better direct their criticisms at forces excluding poor minorities and whites from literate culture, rather than minimizing the value of that culture as some leftists do."

It's not a matter of being for or against Western civilization. We are all victims of it. It's time to consider that the classics may, in fact, make more sense to some of us as records of blindness to the plight of the world's majorities, than as sublime masterpieces. Or as Walter Benjamin once suggested, "There's no document of civilization which is not at the same time a document of barbarism." That doesn't mean, however, that we don't need to read and analyze them. It means that we need to keep our eye on the ball.

The important thing to change is the way minority people lack access to the primary means of social communication at every level from mass media to academic publishing. They neither own nor manage – except in the case of marginal institutions – publishing companies, magazines, television stations, film studios, museums, theaters. "Cultural detention centers" is how Ishmael Reed characterizes their abuse of power in *Mumbo Jumbo*. Blacks are discouraged from service as writers, editors, curators, and directors in these cultural detention centers. As perpetual objects of contemplation, contempt, derision, appropriation, and marginalization, Afro-Americans are kept too busy to ever become producers. Further, the educational system, which doesn't take seriously their educational potential especially as writers, sabotages them from kindergarten to college. Since the Civil Rights revolution, even more so. Either what they have to learn turns them off, or they're turned off by the spirit in which it is offered.

My sister may provide just such a case. She advanced to candidacy in theoretical linguistics seven years ago, then later switched her field to socio-linguistics: black English as spoken by black women in Harlem where she lives. Still, with three small children and teaching full time at a public school in New

York, she's unable to finish. Not coincidentally, she refers to the ill-behaved, mostly black, children at her school as "heathens."

Access is denied from inside the black family as well. Poor, uneducated families may regard intellectual activity as, ipso facto, elitist. Middle-class black families may have the equivalent attitude (especially for girls) regarding advanced intellectual activity as unfeminine, unhealthy, and "white." Education is considered a means to an end – a way to become a doctor or a lawyer or "an Indian chief" – as though it was somehow also completely ridiculous.

Rainbow Coalition of the Mind

But now I know an Indian chief – Wilma Mankiller, the first female chief of the Cherokee Nation in Oklahoma – whose struggle is also a struggle with language and representation. The Cherokee are also invisible to most Americans, even to most Oklahomans, even to most blacks. I've become fascinated by the unwillingness of "American history" to include Oklahoma in its big picture. It's like one of those nuclear dump sites, some place nobody wants to know anything about.

Perhaps it remains this frightening unknown quantity because its population didn't whiten until the 1920s. Years after all the unwanted Native Americans in the Southeast were rounded up and herded to the "Indian Territory," most notably in the Trail of Tears – ex-slaves began to rally there as well because of the rumors that black men were prosperous in the territory – the possibility of Oklahoma entering the union as an Indian or black state was seriously considered.

Native Americans wanted to call the Indian state Sequoyah, after the man who had invented the Cherokee alphabet. He thought the one great advantage whites had over his people was writing. So he set about improving the odds. I don't want to romanticize Cherokee development – the alphabet didn't save them from the hypocrisy of whites. But what strikes me as important about the Cherokees, and all Native American groups, is that they have a different historical relationship to the question of race, and demonstrate another paradigm of assimilation without success. The useful thing might be to make comparisons, to dislodge the phantom fears, to find out what's really there. I can't think why the one thing both American Studies at Yale and at SUNY–Buffalo have in common is a total lack of interest in such questions.

Of course, we all contribute to the dichotomizing of black and white that allows the media to trivialize the Jackson campaign, and which erases again and again American cultural diversity. But I feel as though Sequoyah is a state of mind, the predisposition to regard the United States as a function of American pluralism, a rainbow coalition of great expectations, impossible to meet solely with classical solutions.

MICHAEL VENTURA

Report from El Dorado

To go from a job you don't like to watching a screen on which others live more intensely than you ... is American life, by and large.

This is our political ground. This is our artistic ground. This is what we've done with our immense resources. We have to stop calling it "entertainment" or "news" or "sports" and start calling it what it is: our most immediate environment.

This is a very, very different America from the America that built the industrial capacity to win the Second World War and to surge forward on the multiple momentums of that victory for thirty years. That was an America that worked at mostly menial tasks during the day (now we work at mostly clerical tasks) and had to look at each other at night.

I'm not suggesting a nostalgia for that time. It was repressive and bigoted to an extent that is largely forgotten today, to cite only two of its uglier aspects. But in that environment America meant *America*: the people and the land. The land was far bigger than what we'd done with the land.

This is no longer true. Now the environment of America is media. Not the land itself, but the image of the land. The focus is not on the people so much as it is on the interplay between people and screens. What we've done with the land is far more important now than the land – we're not even dealing with the land anymore, we're dealing with our manipulation and pollution of it.

And what we've done with the very concept of "image" is taking on far more importance for many of us than the actual sights and sounds of our lives.

For instance: Ronald Reagan stands on a cliff in Normandy to commemorate the day U.S. Army Rangers scaled those cliffs in the World War II invasion. Today's Rangers reenact the event while some of the original Rangers, in their sixties now, look on. Except that it is the wrong cliff. The cliff that was actually scaled is a bit further down the beach, but it's not as photogenic as this cliff, so this cliff has been chosen for everybody to emote over. Some of the old Rangers tell reporters that the historical cliff is over yonder, but the old Rangers are swept up (as well they might be) in the ceremonies, and nobody objects enough. This dislocation, this choice, this stance that the real cliff is not important, today's photograph is more important, is a media event. It insults the real event, and overpowers it. Multiplied thousands of times over thousands of outlets of every form and size, ensconced in textbooks as well as screenplays, in sales presentations as well as legislative packages, in religious revivals as well as performance-art pieces, this is the process that has displaced what used to be called "culture."

"I'm not even sure it's a culture anymore. It's like this careening hunger splattering out in all directions."

Jeff Nightbyrd was trying to define "culture" in the wee hours at the Four Queens in Las Vegas. It was a conversation that had been going on since we'd become friends working on the *Austin Sun* in 1974, trying to get our bearings now that the sixties were *really* over. He'd spent that triple-time decade as an SDS organizer and editor of *Rat,* and I'd hit Austin after a few years of road-roving, commune-hopping, and intensive (often depressive) self-exploration – getting by, as the song said, with a little help from my friends, as a lot of us did then. This particular weekend Nightbyrd had come to Vegas from

Austin for a computer convention, and I had taken off from my duties at the *L.A. Weekly* for some lessons in craps (at which Jeff is quite good) and to further our rap. The slot machines clattered around us in unison, almost comfortingly, the way the sound of a large shaky air-conditioner can be comforting in a cheap hotel room when you're trying to remember to forget. We were, after all, trying to fathom an old love: America.

There are worse places to indulge in this obsession than Las Vegas. It is the most American, the most audacious, of cities. Consuming unthinkable amounts of energy in the midst of an unlivable desert (Death Valley is not far away), its decor is based on various cheap-to-luxurious versions of a 1930s Busby Berkeley musical. Indeed, no studio backlot could ever be more of a set, teeming with extras, people who come from all over America, and all over the world, to see the topless, tasteless shows, the Johnny Carson guests on parade doing their utterly predictable routines, the dealers and crap-table croupiers who combine total boredom with ruthless efficiency and milk us dry – yet at least these tourists are risking something they genuinely value: money. It's a quiz show turned into a way of life, where you can get a good Italian dinner at dawn. Even the half-lit hour of the wolf doesn't faze Las Vegas. How could it, when the town has survived the flash of atom bombs tested just over the horizon?

The history books will tell you that, ironically enough, the town was founded by Mormons in 1855. Even their purity of vision couldn't bear the intensity of this desert, and they abandoned the place after just two years. But they had left a human imprint, and a decade later the U.S. Army built a fort here. The settlement hung on, and the railroad came through in 1905. During the Second World War the Mafia started to build the city as we know it now. Religious zealots, the Army, and the Mafia – quite a triad of founding fathers.

Yet one could go back even further, some 400 years, when the first Europeans discovered the deserts of the American West – Spaniards who, as they slowly began to believe that there might be no end to these expansive wilds, became more and more certain that somewhere, somewhere to the north, lay El Dorado – a city of gold. Immeasurable wealth would be theirs, they believed, and eternal youth. What would they have thought if they had suddenly come upon modern Las Vegas, lying as it does in the midst of this bleached nowhere, glowing at night with a brilliance that would have frightened them? We have built our desert city to their measure – for they were gaudy and greedy, devout and vicious, jovial and frenzied, like this town. They had just wasted the entire Aztec civilization because their fantasies were so strong they couldn't see the ancient cultural marvels before their eyes. The Aztecs, awed and terrified, believed they were being murdered by gods; and in the midst of such strangeness, the Spaniards took on godlike powers even in their own eyes. As many Europeans would in America, they took liberties here they would never have taken within sight of their home cathedrals. Their hungers dominated them, and in their own eyes the New World seemed as inexhaustible as their appetites. So when Nightbyrd described our present culture as "a careening hunger splattering out in all directions," he was also, if unintentionally, speaking about our past. Fittingly, we were sitting in the midst of a city that had been fantasized by those seekers of El Dorado 400 years ago. In that sense, America had Las Vegas a century before it had Plymouth Rock. And our sensibility has been caught between the fantasies of the conquistadors and the obsessions of the Puritans ever since.

Yes, a fitting place to try to think about American culture.

"There are memories of culture," Nightbyrd was saying, "but the things that have given people strength have dissolved. And because they're dissolved, people are into distractions. And distractions aren't culture."

Are there even memories? The media have taken over our memories. That day Nightbyrd had been driving through the small towns that dot this desert, towns for which Vegas is only a dull glow to the southwest. In a bar in one of those towns, "like that little bar in *The Right Stuff*," he'd seen pictures of cowboys on the wall. "Except that they weren't cowboys. They were movie stars. Guys who grew up in Glendale [John Wayne] and Santa Monica [Robert Redford]." Surely this desert had its own heroes once, in the old gold-mining towns where a few people still hang on, towns like Goldfield and Tonopah. Remembering those actual heroes would be "culture." Needing pictures of movie stars for want of the real thing is only a nostalgia for culture.

Nostalgia is not memory. Memory is specific. One has a relationship to a memory, and it may be a difficult relationship, because a memory always makes a demand upon the present. But nostalgia is vague, a sentimental wash that obscures memory and acts as a narcotic to dull the importance of the present.

Media as we know it now thrives on nostalgia and is hostile to memory. In a television bio-pic, Helen Keller is impersonated by Mare Winningham. But the face of Helen Keller was marked by her enormous powers of concentration, while the face of Mare Winningham is merely cameo-pretty. A memory has been stolen. It takes a beauty in you to see the beauty in Helen Keller's face, while to cast the face of a Mare Winningham in the role is to suggest, powerfully, that one can come back from the depths unscathed. No small delusion is being sold here. Yet this is a minor instance in a worldwide, twenty-four-hour-a-day onslaught.

An onslaught that gathers momentum every twenty-four hours. Remember that what drew us to Las Vegas was a computer fair. One of these new computers does interesting things with photographs. You can put a photograph into the computer digitally. This means the photograph is in there without a negative or print, each element of the image stored separately. In the computer, you can change any element of the photograph you wish, replacing it or combining it with elements from other photographs. In other words, you can take composites of different photographs and put them into a new photograph of your own composition. Combine this with computer drawing, and you can touch up shadows that don't match. When it comes out of the computer the finished product bears no evidence of tampering with any negative. The possibilities for history books and news stories are infinite. Whole new histories can now be written. Events which never happened can be fully documented.

The neo-Nazis who are trying to convince people that the Holocaust never happened will be able to show the readers of their newsletter an Auschwitz of well-fed, happy people being watched over by kindly S.S. men while tending gardens. And they will be able to make the accusation that photographs of the *real* Auschwitz were created in a computer by manipulative Jews. The Soviet Union can rewrite Czechoslovakia and Afghanistan, the United States can rewrite Vietnam, and atomic weapons proponents can prove that the average resident of Hiroshima was unharmed by the blast. On a less sinister, but equally disruptive, level, the writers of business prospectuses and real-estate brochures can have a field day.

Needless to say, when any photograph can be processed this way then all photographs become suspect. It not only becomes easier to lie, it becomes far harder to tell the truth.

But why should this seem shocking when under the names of "entertainment" and "advertising" we've been filming history, and every facet of daily life, in just this way for nearly a century now? It shouldn't surprise us that the ethics of our entertainment have taken over, and that we are viewing reality itself as a form of entertainment. And, as entertainment, reality can be rewritten, transformed, played with, in any fashion.

These considerations place us squarely at the center of our world – and we have no choice, it's the only world there is anymore. *Electronic media has done for everyday reality what Einstein did for physics:* everything is shifting. Even the shifts are shifting. And a fact is not so crucial anymore, not so crucial as the process that turns a fact into an image. For we live now with images as much as facts, and the images seem to impart more life than facts *precisely because they are so capable of transmutation, of transcendence, able to transcend their sources and their uses.* And all the while the images goad us on, so that we become partly images ourselves, imitating the properties of images as we surround ourselves with images.

This is most blatant in our idea of "a vacation" – an idea only about 100 years old. To "vacation" is to enter an image. Las Vegas is only the most shrill embodiment of this phenomenon. People come here not so much to gamble (individual losses are comparatively light), nor for the glittery entertainment, but to step into an image, a daydream, a filmlike world where "everything" is promised. No matter that the Vegas definition of "everything" is severely limited, what thrills tourists is the sense of being surrounded in "real life" by the same images that they see on TV. But the same is true of the Grand Canyon, or Yellowstone National Park, or Yosemite, or Death Valley, or virtually any of our "natural" attractions. What with all their roads, telephones, bars, cable-TV motels, the visitors are carefully protected from having to *experience* the place. They view its image, they camp out in its image, ski down or climb up its image, take deep breaths of its image, let its image give them a tan. Or, when they tour the cities, they ride the quaint trolley cars of the city's image, they visit the Latin Quarter of its image, they walk across the Brooklyn Bridge of its image – our recreation is a *re*-creation of America into one big Disneyland.

And this is only one way we have stripped the very face of America of any content, any reality, concentrating only on its power as image. We also elect images, groom ourselves as images, make an image of our home, our car, and now, with aerobics, of our very bodies. For in the aerobics craze the flesh becomes a garment, susceptible to fashion. So it becomes less *our* flesh, though the exercise may make it more serviceable. It becomes "my" body, like "my" car, "my" house. What, within us, is saying "my"? What is transforming body into image? We shy away from asking. In this sense it can be said that after the age of about twenty-five we no longer *have* bodies anymore – we have possessions that are either more or less young, which we are constantly trying to transform and through which we try to breathe.

It's not that all this transformation of realities into un- or

non- or supra-realities is "bad," but that it's unconscious, com-
pulsive, reductive. We rarely make things more than they
were; we simplify them into less. Though surely the process
could – at least theoretically – go both ways. Or so India's
meditators and Zen's monks say. But that would be to *increase*
meaning, and we seem bent on the elimination of meaning.
We're Reagan's Rangers, climbing a cliff that *is* a real cliff,
except it's not the cliff we say it is, so that the meaning of both
cliffs – not to mention of our act of climbing – is reduced.

As I look out onto a glowing city that is more than 400
years old but was built only during the last forty years, as I
watch it shine in blinking neon in a desert that has seen the
flash of atom bombs, it becomes more and more plain to me
that America is at war with meaning. America is form opposed to content. Not just form *instead* of content. Form
opposed. Often violently. There are few things resented so
much among us as the suggestion that what we do *means*. It
means something to watch so much TV. It *means* something to
be obsessed with sports. It *means* something to vacation by
indulging in images. It means something, and therefore it has
consequences. Other cultures have argued over their meanings. We tend to deny that there is any such thing, insisting
instead that what you see is what you get and that's *it*. All
we're doing is having a *good time,* all we're doing is making a
buck, all we're doing is enjoying the spectacle, we insist. So
that when we export American culture what we are really
exporting is an attitude toward content. Media is the American war on content with all the stops out, with meaning in
utter rout, frightened nuances dropping their weapons as
they run.

"Media is the history that forgives," my friend Dave Johnson
told me on a drive through that same desert a few months
later. We love to take a weekend every now and again and just
drive. Maybe it started with reading *On the Road* when we were
kids, or watching a great old TV show called *Route 66* about
two guys who drove from town to town working at odd jobs

and having adventures with intense women who, when asked who they were, might say (as one did), "Suppose I said I was the Queen of Spain?" Or maybe it was all those rock 'n' roll songs about "the road" – the road, where we can blast our tape-decks as loud as we want, and watch the world go by without having to touch it, a trip through the greatest hologram there is, feeling like neither boys nor men but both and something more, embodiments of some ageless, restless principle of movement rooted deep in our prehistory. All of which is to say that we're just as stuck with the compulsion to enter the image as anybody, and that we love the luxuries of fossil fuel just as much as any other red-blooded, thickheaded Americans.

Those drives are our favorite time to talk, and, again, America is our oldest flame. We never tire of speaking of her, nor of our other old girlfriends. For miles and miles of desert I thought of what Dave had said.

"Media is the history that forgives." A lovely way to put it, and quite un-Western. We Westerners tend to think in sets of opposites: good/bad, right/wrong, me/you, past/present. These sets are often either antagonistic (East/West, commie/ capitalist, Christian/heathen) or they set up a duality that instantly calls out to be bridged (man/woman). But Dave's comment sidesteps the dualities and suggests something more complex: a lyrical impulse is alive somewhere in all this media obfuscation. It is the impulse to redeem the past – in his word, to *forgive* history – by presenting it as we would have most liked it to be.

It is one thing to accuse the media of lying. They are, and they know it, and they know we know, and we know they know that we know, and nothing changes. It is another to recognize the rampant lying shallowness of our media as a massive united longing for ... innocence? For a sheltered childlike state in which we need not know about our world or our past. We are so desperate for this that we are willing to accept ignorance as a substitute for innocence. For there can be no doubt anymore that this society *knowingly* accepts its ignorance as innocence – we have seen so much in the last twenty years that now we know what we *don't* see. Whenever a TV show or a movie or a news broadcast leaves out crucial realities for the sake of sentimentality, we pretty much understand the nature of what's been left out and why.

But American media *forgives* the emptiness and injustice of our daily life by presenting our daily life as innocent. Society, in turn, forgives American media for lying because if we accept the lie as truth then we needn't *do* anything, we needn't change.

I like Dave's line of thought because it suggests a motive – literally, a motive force – for these rivers of glop that stream from the screens and loudspeakers of our era. Because, contrary to popular belief, profit is *not* the motive. That seems a rash statement to make in the vicinity of Las Vegas, but the profit motive merely begs the question: *why* is it profitable? Profit, in media, is simply a way of measuring attention. Why does what we call "media" attract so much attention?

The answer is that it is otherwise too crippling for individuals to bear the strain of accepting the unbalanced, unrewarding, uninspiring existence that is advertised as "normal daily life" for most people who have to earn a living every day.

Do those words seem too strong? Consider: to go to a job you don't value in itself but for its paycheck, while your kids go to a school that is less and less able to educate them; a large percentage of your pay is taken by the government for defenses that don't defend, welfare that doesn't aid, and the upkeep of a government that is impermeable to the influence of a single individual; while you are caught in a value system that judges you by what you own, in a society where it is taken for granted now that children can't communicate with their parents, that old people have to be shut away in homes, and that no neighborhood is *really* safe; while the highest medical costs in the world don't prevent us from having one of the worst health records in the West (for instance, New York has a far higher infant mortality rate than Hong Kong), and the air, water, and supermarket food are filled with God-knows-what; and to have, at the end of a busy yet uneventful life, little to show for enduring all this but a comfortable home if you've "done well" enough; yet to *know* all along that you're living in the freest, most powerful country in the world, though you haven't had time to exercise much freedom and don't personally have any power – this is to be living a life of slow attrition and maddening contradictions.

Add to this a social style that values cheerfulness more than any other attribute, and then it is not so strange or shocking that the average American family watches six to eight hours of network television a day. It is a cheap and sanctioned way to partake of this world without having actually to live in it.

Certainly they don't watch so much TV because they're bored – there's far too much tension in their lives to call them bored, and, in fact, many of the products advertised on their favorite programs feature drugs to calm them down. Nor is it because they're stupid – a people managing the most technically intricate daily life in history can hardly be written off as stupid; nor because they can't entertain themselves – they are not so different from the hundreds of generations of their forebears who entertained themselves very well as a matter of course. No, they are glued to the TV because one of the most fundamental messages of television is: "It's all right."

Every sitcom and drama says: "It's all right." Those people on the tube go through the same – if highly stylized – frustrations, and are exposed to the same dangers as we are, yet they reappear magically every week (every day on the soap operas) ready for more, always hopeful, always cheery, never questioning the fundamental premise that this is the way a great culture behaves and that all the harassments are the temporary inconveniences of a beneficent society. It's going to get even *better*, but even now *it's all right.* The commercials, the Hollywood movies, the universal demand in every television drama or comedy that no character's hope can ever be exhausted, combine in a deafening chorus of: *It's all right.*

As a screenwriter I have been in many a film production meeting, and not once have I heard any producer or studio executive say, "We have to lie to the public." What I have heard, over and over, is, "They have to leave the theater feeling good." This, of course, easily (though not always) translates into lying – into simplifying emotions and events so that "it's all right." You may measure how deeply our people know "it" is *not* all right, not at all, by how much money they are willing to pay to be ceaselessly told that it is. The more they feel it's not, the more they need to be told it is – hence Mr. Reagan's popularity.

Works that don't say "It's all right" don't get much media attention or make much money.

The culture itself is in the infantile position of needing to be assured, every day, all day, that this way of life is good for you. Even the most disturbing news is dispensed in the most reassuring package. As world news has gotten more and more disturbing, the trend in broadcast journalism has been to get more and more flimflam, to take it less seriously, to keep up the front of "It's really quite all right." This creates an enormous tension between the medium and its messages, because everybody knows that what's on the news is *not* all right. That is why such big money is paid to a newscaster with a calm, authoritative air who, by his presence alone, seems to resolve the contradictions of his medium. Walter Cronkite was the most popular newscaster in broadcast history because his very presence implied: "As long as I'm on the air, you can be sure that, no matter what I'm telling you, *it's still all right.*"

Which is to say that the media has found it profitable to do the mothering of the mass psyche. But it's a weak mother. It cannot nurture. All it can do is say it's all right, tuck us in, and hope for the best.

Today most serious, creative people exhaust themselves in a sideline commentary on this state of affairs, a commentary that usually gets sucked up into the media and spewed back out in a format that says "It's all right. What this guy's saying is quite all right, what this woman's singing is all right, all right." This is what "gaining recognition" virtually always means now in America: your work gets turned inside out so that its meaning becomes "It's all right."

Of course, most of what exists *to make media of,* to make images of, is more and more disorder. Media keeps saying, "It's all right" while being fixated upon the violent, the chaotic, and the terrifying. So the production of media becomes more and more schizoid, with two messages simultaneously being broadcast: "It's all right. We're dying. It's all right. We're all dying." The other crucial message – "We're dying" – runs right alongside *It's all right.*

Murder is the crux of much media "drama." But it's murder presented harmlessly, with trivial causes cited. Rare is the attempt, in all our thousands of murder dramas, to delve below the surface. We take for granted now, almost as an immutable principle of dramatic unity, that significant numbers of us want to kill significant numbers of the rest of us. And what are all the murders in our media but a way of saying "We are being killed, we are killing, we are dying"? Only a people dying and in the midst of death would need to see so much of it in such sanitized form *in order to make death harmless.* This is the way we choose to share our death.

Delete the word "entertainment" and say instead, North Americans devote an enormous amount of time to the ritual of sharing death. If this were recognized as a ritual, and if the deaths were shared with a respect for the realities and the mysteries of death, this might be a very useful thing to do. But there is no respect for death in our death-dependent media, there is only the compulsion to display death. As for the consumers, they consume these deaths like sugar pills. Their ritual goes on far beneath any level on which they'd be prepared to admit the word "ritual." So we engage in a ritual we pretend isn't happening, hovering around deaths that we say aren't real.

It is no coincidence that this practice has thrived while the Pentagon uses the money of these death watchers to create weapons for death on a scale that is beyond the powers of human imagination – the very same human imagination that is stunting itself by watching ersatz deaths, as though intentionally crippling its capacity to envision the encroaching dangers. It is possible that the Pentagon's process could not go on without the dulling effects of this "entertainment."

When we're not watching our screens, we're listening to music. And, of course, North Americans listen to love songs at every possible opportunity, through every possible orifice of media. People under the strain of such dislocating unrealities need to hear "I love you, I love you," as often as they can. "I love you" or "I used to love you" or "I ought to love you" or "I need to love you" or "I want to love you." It is the fashion of pop-music critics to discount the words for the style, forgetting that most of the world's cultures have had songs about *everything*, songs about work, about the sky, about death, about the gods, about getting up in the morning, about animals, about children, about eating, about dreams – about everything, along with love. These were songs that everybody knew and sang. For a short time in the late sixties we moved toward such songs again, but that was a brief digression; since the First World War the music that most North Americans listen to has been a music of love lyrics that rarely go beyond adolescent yearnings. Either the song is steeped in the yearnings themselves, or it is saturated with a longing for the days when one could, shamelessly, feel like an adolescent. The beat has changed radically from decade to decade, but with brief exceptions that beat has carried the same pathetic load. (The beat, thankfully, has given us other gifts.)

It can't be over-emphasized that these are entertainments of a people whose basic imperative is the need not to think about their environment. The depth of their need may be measured by the hysterical popularity of this entertainment; it is also the measure of how little good it does them.

Media is not experience. In its most common form, media substitutes a fantasy of experience or (in the case of news) an abbreviation of experience for the living fact. But in our culture the absorption of media has become a substitute for experience. We absorb media, we don't live it – there is a vast psychological difference, and it is a difference that is rarely brought up.

For example, in the 1940s, when one's environment was still one's *environment,* an experience to be lived instead of a media-saturation to be absorbed, teenagers like Elvis Presley and Jerry Lee Lewis didn't learn their music primarily from the radio. Beginning when they were small boys they sneaked over to the black juke joints of Louisiana and Mississippi and Tennessee, where they weren't supposed to go, and they listened and learned. When Lewis and Presley began recording, even though they were barely twenty they had tremendous authority because they had experience – a raw experience of crossing foreign boundaries, of streets and sounds and peoples, of the night-to-night learning of ways that could not be taught at home.

This is very different from young musicians now who learn from a product, not a living ground. Their music doesn't get to them till it's been sifted through elaborate corporate networks of production and distribution. It doesn't smack of the raw world that exists before "product" can even be thought of.

The young know this, of course. They sense the difference intensely, and often react to it violently. So white kids from suburban media culture invented slam dancing (jumping up and down and slamming into each other) while black kids from the South Bronx, who have to deal with realities far more urgent than media, were elaborating the astounding graces of break dancing.

Slam dancing was a dead end. Break dancing, coming from a living ground, goes out through media but becomes ultimately transformed into another living ground – the kids in the elementary school down the street in Santa Monica break dance. Which is to say, a grace has been added to their lives. A possibility of grace. With the vitality that comes from having originated from a living ground. The media here is taking its proper role as a channel, not as a world in itself. It's possible that these kids are being affected more in their bodies and their daily lives by the South Bronx subculture than by high-gloss films like *Gremlins* or *Indiana Jones and the Temple of Doom*. Even through all this static, life can speak to life.

Of course, break dancing inevitably gets hyped, and hence devalued, by the entertainment industry, the way Elvis Presley ended up singing "Viva Las Vegas" as that town's most glamorous headliner. He went from being the numinous son of a living ground to being the charismatic product of a media empire – the paradigm of media's power to transform the transformers. The town veritably glows in the dark with the strength of media's mystique.

We do not yet know what life *is* in a media environment. We have not yet evolved a contemporary culture that can supply the definition – or rather, supply the constellation of concepts in which that definition would live and grow. These seem such simple statements, but they are at the crux of the American dilemma now. An important aspect of this dilemma is that we've barely begun a body of thought and art which is focused on what is really *alive* in the ground of a media-saturated daily life. For culture always proceeds from two poles: one is the people of the land and the street; the other is the thinker. You see this most starkly in revolutions: the ground swell on the one hand, the thinker (the Jefferson, for instance) on the other. Or religiously, the ground swell of belief that is articulated by a Michelangelo or a Dante. The two poles can exist without each other but they cannot be effective without each other.

Unless a body of thought connects with a living ground, there is no possibility that this era will discover itself within its cacophony and create, one day, a post-A.D. culture. It is ours to attempt the thought and seek the ground – for all of us exist between those poles. We are not only dying. We are living. And we are struggling to share our lives, which is all, finally, that "culture" means.

Opening the American Mind

A PRELIMINARY LIST

E. D. Hirsch, Jr., Joseph Kett, and James Trefil, all of whom are professors at the University of Virginia, Charlottesville, compiled, for inclusion in Hirsch's book, *Cultural Literacy*, a list they called "What Literate Americans Know." They admitted that the list was preliminary and provisional, and added a few things to the list for the paperback printing of the book. Their list included approximately 5,000 names, dates, places, phrases, terms, and concepts that they believe knowledgeable citizens should know.

Rick Simonson and Scott Walker, editors of *The Graywolf Annual 5: Multi-Cultural Literacy*, think the list compiled by Hirsch and his colleagues is fine as far as it goes, but that their list is alarmingly deficient in its male and European bias.

The brief list printed below is intended only to suggest the sorts of things not included in the Hirsch book, the sorts of things too commonly excluded from U.S. educational texts, political thinking, or social planning. The list could be considerably lengthened, and we prefer to think of this list as simply the start of a discussion among friends who hope to improve the educational system of this country, and to make its citizens more aware of the important roles played in our lives by a great many cultures.

THE LIST

100,000 Songs of Milarepa
AA (Alcoholics Anonymous)
AAA (American Automobile
   Association)
Abdul-Jabbar, Kareem
aborigine
abstract expressionism
Absurd, Theater of the
Achebe, Chinua
ACOA (Adult Children of
   Alcoholics)
action painting
Ade, King Sunny
Adler, Alfred
adobe
advertising
African diaspora
Afro-American
Agent Orange
Akhmatova, Anna
Al-Anon
alcoholism
Allende, Salvador
alphabet
altar
Amado, Jorge
amen
Anasazi (tribe)
ancestor worship

anima/animus
anthology
antiwar movement
apse
aquaculture
Aquarius
Arabic
Arafat, Yasir
Aries
Art Deco
Ashé
ashram
Asian Exclusion Act
attention span
Baal
Baha'i
Baja California
Baldwin, James
Bannister, Roger
barrio
Bartók, Béla
Bashō
Batman
Bay of Bengal
Beamon, Bob
beat, the
beatnick
Beckett, Samuel
Belize

Bell's Theorem
Benedict, Ruth
Bergman, Ingmar
Bhagavad Gita
Biko, Steve
bilingual
biodegradable
biological clock
biopsy
bioregional
birds and the bees, the
Black and Tans
Black Elk
Bloody Sunday
bluegrass (music)
Bly, Robert
Bogotá
Bolívar, Simón
Bonhoeffer, Dietrich
boom box
boot up
Borges, Jorge Luis
braille
Brecht, Bertolt
Breton, André
Bringing in the Sheaves
    (song)
Brodsky, Joseph
Brooks, Gwendolyn
Buchenwald
Buñuel, Luis
Cage, John
Cajun
Campbell, Joseph
Camus, Albert
Capone, Al
Capricorn

Cardenal, Ernesto
Carver, George Washington
Castaneda, Carlos
Castro Street
cathouse
cause and effect
Cavafy, Constantine
Cavell, Edith
celibacy
Celtic
Chandler, Raymond
chaos (sci. term)
charge
Charlotte's Web (title)
chautauqua
Chernobyl
chess
Cheyenne (tribe)
child abuse
Chinese New Year
chiropractic
cholera
Chopin, Kate
Christian radicalism
church
Cinco de Mayo
Cinderella
cinéma verité
clan
co-parenting
Cochise
codependency
Cole, Nat King
Colette
community
condom
cool (personality attribute)

corporate/party line
corruption
Cosby, Bill
covert operations
Coyote
crash (computer)
cultural materialism
cybernetics
dadaism
Damballah
Dar-es-Salaam
Davis, Miles
de Beauvoir, Simone
Decline and Fall of the
    Roman Empire, The (title)
deep ecology
defoliation
Dhammapada
Diamond Sutra
diaspora
Díaz del Castillo, Bernal
Díaz, Porfirio
Diddley, Bo
Dinesen, Isak
Disappeared, The
disinformation
divorce
Dixieland jazz
Djakarta
domestic violence
dope
downtime
down under
Dr. J
Dresden
Druids
drum

dub poetry
Earhart, Amelia
Easter Island
Easter, 1916
economic violence
El Salvador
Elegba
Elytis, Odysseus
endangered species
environmental impact
    statement
environmental movement
Evers, Medgar
extinction
facts of life
fallout
Farsi
fax
fertility
film noir
Fonda, Jane
football
FORTRAN
Franklin, Aretha
Freud, Anna
Friedan, Betty
Fromm, Erich
fructose
Fuentes, Carlos
funk
Gaia hypothesis
García Lorca, Federico
García Márquez, Gabriel
Gaye, Marvin
Gemini
genitals
get down

Gesundheit
ghost dance
Gide, André
gift
Gilgamesh
Ginsberg, Allen
Golden Bough, The (title)
Gorbachev, Mikhail
gospel (music)
Grass, Günter
Great Mother
Green party/movement
Greenpeace
griot
Guadalajara
Guarani (tribe)
Guatemala
Guevara, Che
gulag
gynecology
Haida (tribe)
Hall, Radclyffe
Halloween
Hamburger Hill
Hamilton, Edith
Hansberry, Lorraine (Raisin
    in the Sun)
Happy Birthday (song)
Harlem Renaissance
Hasidic
Health Maintenance
    Organization
Heaney, Seamus
Heaven
Hebrew
Hell
Hidalgo, Miguel

History is bunk
Holiday, Billie
homeopathy
homophobia
Hopi
hostile takeover
Hughes, Langston
Hurston, Zora Neale
Hydra
hyperspace
hysterectomy
I Ching
I heard it through the grape
    vine
I will fight no more forever
Ibn al-'Arabī
"If you want to see a mask
    dancing, you cannot stand
    in one place." – Ibo
    proverb
Inanna
indigenous
Indonesia
infertility
infiltration
instant replay
internment camps
Inuit (tribe)
Isis
issei
It ain't me, babe
Ivory Coast
Iztapalapa
jam session
jazz-rock fusion (music)
Jeffers, Robinson
jit (music)

jive
Johnson, Robert
joint custody
Jones, Mother
Jones, Quincy
juju music
Kaballah
Kahlo, Frida
Kalahari Desert
Kali
karma
Kawabata, Yasunari
Kenya
Kerouac, Jack
Khmer Rouge
Killing Fields
Kiowa (tribe)
kiva
Krishna
kundalini yoga
Kundera, Milan
Kung (tribe)
Kurosawa, Akira
Kyoto
Lagos
land ethic
land stewardship
Lao Tzu
Laveau, Marie
Lawrence, Jacob
learning disability
Lem, Stanislaw
Leo
Lessing, Doris
Li Po
liberation theology
Libra

Little Red Book, The
Lone Ranger
loom (weaver's)
Los Alamos, New Mexico
Love Canal
Mabinogion, The
macrobiotic
magical realism
Magritte, René
Maharishi Mahesh Yogi
makossa (music)
Mandela, Nelson
Marley, Bob
mastectomy
mbaqanga (music)
McCarthy, Joseph
McCoy, Elijah
McCullers, Carson
Mead, Margaret
Means, Russell
Mekong Delta
mercenary soldier
mestizo
Middle Passage
migrant worker
Milarepa
military-industrial complex
Millett, Kate
Mingus, Charles
Mishima, Yukio
misogyny
Mistral, Gabriella
modem
Monk, Meredith
monocultural
monolingual
Montale, Eugenio

prayer
premenstrual syndrome
prime time
prison
prophylactic
prostitution
protein debt
provincial
psyche
public relations
pueblo
Puget Sound
Puig, Manuel
put to bed (finish)
Quetzalcoatl
quilt
racial slur
Rainbow Coalition
randomness (sci. term)
rap (music)
rape
Rasta
Ray, Man
recycling
Reed, Ishmael
reforestation
refusenik
reggae
REM (rapid eye movement)
reservation (Indian)
retrograde
revolution
Rexroth, Kenneth
rhythm and blues (music)
Rich, Adrienne
riff
right brain/left brain

Rilke, Rainer Maria
rock 'n' roll
Rome
Rumi
safe sex
Sagittarius
samba
Sand Creek
Sandinismo
Sands, Bobby
Sanger, Margaret
sansei
scat
Seattle, Chief
selective perception
semiotics
sexism
shadow (psychological term)
shaman
shaman(ism)
shango
Shinto
Shiva
ska (music)
Smith, Bessie
Smokey the Bear
Snyder, Gary
soca music
soccer
socialized medicine
socially responsible investing
solar energy
Solidarity movement
Somoza
Sonoran Desert
soukous (music)
soul

soul food
soul music
Souls of Black Folk, The
    (title)
Soweto, South Africa
Soyinka, Wole
spirituals (music)
Springsteen, Bruce
St. Patrick's Day
strange particles
Stuart Little (title)
subatomic particles
substance abuse
sucrose
Sufi
supercomputers
supply and demand, law of
sustained yield agriculture
sutra
Swahili
synchronicity
Synge, John M.
synthetic
Tagalog
Tao Te Ching
Tarot
Taurus
telephone
television
Tenochtitlan
terminate with extreme
    prejudice
Tex-Mex (music)
Tharp, Twyla
thunder
tide
Tierra del Fuego

Tillich, Paul
Tlingit
Tonto
Toomer, Jean
toxic
trade deficit
Treblinka
tribe
trickster
Truffaut, François
Truth, Sojourner
Tsvetaeva, Marina
Tu Fu
Tutu, Desmond
Uinta Mountains
underworld
Undset, Sigrid
United Fruit Company
Upanishads
Ural Mountains
Uruguay
Valentine's Day
vegetarian(ism)
Vietnam War Memorial
Villa, Francisco (Pancho)
Villa-Lobos, Heitor
virgin forest
Virgo
vodun (Voodoo, Hoodoo,
    etc.)
Walbiri (tribe)
Walesa, Lech
Walker, Alice
war-tax resistance
warlock
wars of liberation
Waters, Muddy

weaving
Welty, Eudora
White Supremacy
White, E. B.
Wicce
Wilder, Laura Ingalls
wilderness
Williams, William Carlos
witchcraft
Wobblies
Wolf, Howlin'

Wollstonecraft, Mary
Wounded Knee
Yeats, William Butler
Yiddish
yoga
Yoruba
Zaire
Zimbabwe
Zohar
zombie
Zulu

ENDNOTES

Who Is Your Mother?
Red Roots of White Feminism

1. The White Roots of Peace, cited in *The Third Woman: Minority Women Writers of the United States*, ed. Dexter Fisher (Boston: Houghton Mifflin, 1980), p. 577. Cf. Thomas Sanders and William Peek, eds., *Literature of the American Indian* (New York: Glencoe Press, 1973), pp. 208–239. Sanders and Peek refer to the document as "The Law of the Great Peace."

2. Stan Steiner, *The New Indians* (New York: Dell, 1968), pp. 219–220.

3. William Brandon, *The Last Americans: The Indian in American Culture* (New York: McGraw-Hill, 1974), p. 294.

4. Brandon, *Last Americans*, p. 6.

5. Brandon, *Last Americans*, pp. 7–9. The entire chapter "American Indians and American History" (pp. 1–23) is pertinent to the discussion.

6. Ella E. Clark and Margot Evans, *Sacagawea of the Lewis and Clark Expedition* (Berkeley: University of California Press, 1979), pp. 93–98. Clark details the fascinating, infuriating, and very funny scholarly escapade of how our suffragette foremothers created a feminist hero from the scant references to the teenage Shoshoni wife of the expedition's official translator, Pierre Charbonneau.

7. The implications of this maneuver did not go unnoticed by either whites or Indians, for the statues of the idealized Shoshoni woman, the Native American matron Sacagawea, suggest that American tenure on American land, indeed, the right to be on this land, is given to whites by her. While that implication is not overt, it certainly is suggested in the image of her that the sculptor chose: a tall, heavy woman, standing erect, nobly pointing the way westward with upraised hand. The impression is furthered by the habit of media and scholar of referring to her as "the guide." Largely because of the popularization of the circumstances of Sacagawea's participation in the famed Lewis and Clark expedition, Indian people have viewed her as a traitor to her people, likening her to Malinalli (La Malinche, who acted as interpreter for Cortés and bore him a son) and Pocahontas, that unhappy girl who married John Rolfe (not John Smith) and died in England after bearing him a son. Actually none of these women engaged in traitorous behavior. Sacagawea led a long life, was called Porivo (Chief Woman) by the Comanches, among whom she lived for more than twenty years, and in her old age

engaged her considerable skill at speaking and manipulating white bureaucracy to help in assuring her Shoshoni people decent reservation holdings.

A full discussion is impossible here but an examination of American childrearing practices, societal attitudes toward women and exhibited by women (when compared to the same in Old World cultures) as well as the foodstuffs, medicinal materials, countercultural and alternative cultural systems, and the deeply Indian values these reflect should demonstrate the truth about informal acculturation and cross-cultural connections in the Americas.

8. Brandon, *Last Americans,* p. 6.

9. Lewis Henry Morgan, *Ancient Society or Researches in the Lines of Human Progress from Savagery Through Barbarism to Civilization* (New York, 1877).

10. Clark and Evans, *Sacagawea,* p. 96.

Tlilli, Tlapalli: The Path of the Red and Black Ink

1. R. Gordon Wasson, *The Wondrous Mushroom: Mycolatry in Mesoamerica* (New York, NY: McGraw-Hill Book Company, 1980), 59, 103.

2. Robert Plant Armstrong, *The Powers of Presence: Consciousness, Myth, and Affecting Presence* (Philadelphia, PA: University of Pennsylvania Press, 1981), 11, 20.

3. Armstrong, 10.

4. Armstrong, 4.

5. Miguel Leon-Portilla, *Los Antiguos Mexicanos: A través de sus crónicas y cantares* (México, D.F.: Fondo de Cultura Económica, 1961), 19, 22.

6. Leon-Portilla, 125.

7. In *Xóchitl* in *Cuícatl* is Nahuatl for flower and song, *flor y canto.*

8. Nietzsche, in *The Will to Power,* says that the artist lives under a curse of being vampirized by his talent.

CONTRIBUTORS

PAULA GUNN ALLEN's book, *The Sacred Hoop: Recovering the Feminine in American Indian Traditions*, was published in 1986. She is one of the foremost Native American literary critics and has published several books of poetry and a novel, *The Woman Who Owned the Shadows*.

GLORIA ANZALDÚA is a contributing editor of *Sinister Wisdom*. Her book, *Borderlands/La Frontera: The New Mestiza*, was published in 1987 and explores her Spanish and Indian heritage in both prose and poetry.

JAMES BALDWIN is well known for his novels, among them – *Go Tell It on the Mountain* and *Another Country*, but it is his essay collections – *Notes of a Native Son, Nobody Knows My Name, The Price of the Ticket*, and *The Fire Next Time* – which made him a spokesman for the civil rights movement. After living for many years as an expatriate, he died in 1987 in the south of France.

WENDELL BERRY is a farmer and a writer, with numerous novels, books of poetry, and essay collections to his name. "People, Land, and Community" was taken from *Standing by Words: Essays*, published in 1983.

MICHELLE CLIFF's latest book, featuring both poems and prose, is *The Land of Look Behind*. She was born in Kingston, Jamaica, educated in London, and now lives in California.

CARLOS FUENTES is currently Professor of Latin American Studies at Harvard University. His collection of essays, *Myself with Others*, was published in 1988. An essayist and a political writer, he has also published many novels, including *Terra Nostra* and *The Death of Artemio Cruz*.

EDUARDO GALEANO is an Uruguayan writer and editor who recently returned to his country after nearly a decade in exile. The essay here is taken from his memoir, *Days and Nights of Love and War*. His trilogy, *Memories of Fire*, has been published to wide acclaim.

GUILLERMO GÓMEZ-PEÑA is a visual artist living in San Diego, California. His essay was taken from the *L.A. Weekly*.

DAVID MURA's essay is from a yet unpublished book, *Turning Japanese*. He was a U.S./Japan Fellowship winner and spent a year living and traveling in Japan. His book of poetry, *After We Lost Our Way*, will be published as part of the National Poetry Series in 1989.

ISHMAEL REED is the editorial director of Yardbird Press and a contributing writer to the *New York Times, Los Angeles Times, Black Words*, and *Ramparts*. He has published many novels, including *Flight to Canada* and *Mumbo Jumbo*. His latest book is *Writin' Is Fightin'*, a collection of critical essays and reviews.

MICHAEL VENTURA's latest book, *Shadow Dancing in the U.S.A.*, a collection of essays taken from his columns in the *L.A. Weekly*, was published in 1985.

MICHELE WALLACE's book *Black Macho and the Myth of the Superwoman* was published in 1979. She is a frequent contributor to *Ms., Esquire*, and *Mother Jones*.